Schools and Communities

Working together to transform children's lives

John West-Burnham, Maggie Farrar
and George Otero

network
continuum

Published by Network Continuum Education
The Tower Building
11 York Road
London
SE1 7NX

www.networkcontinuum.co.uk
www.continuumbooks.com

An imprint of The Continuum International Publishing Group Ltd

First published 2007
© John West-Burnham, Maggie Farrar and George Otero 2007

ISBN-13: 978 1 85539 233 5
ISBN-10:   1 85539 233 X

Managing editor: Dawn Booth
Layout by: Neil Hawkins, ndesign
Cover design by: The Oak Studio Limited
Illustrations by: Dave Thompson

Printed in Great Britain by MPG Books Ltd, Bodmin, Cornwall

Contents

Introduction

This book grows out of workshops developed and presented by the authors in association with the Center for RelationaLearning, Santa Fe, New Mexico, and the National College for School Leadership (NCSL) in England, which were held throughout 2004 and 2005. The workshops have also been presented in Australia. The authors are grateful to all those who have attended the workshops who, have enhanced our understanding of the relationship between education and the community.

This book argues for a change of focus in the strategies that are being used to maximize the achievement of every child. The long-term emphasis on school improvement has been very successful in many respects and has had a demonstrable impact on school standards. However, it may now be appropriate to raise the questions to what extent this improvement can be sustained and how much capacity is there to raise standards for all children given that increasing investment and effort do not seem to be producing commensurate outcomes? There is a case for arguing that results at national levels are 'plateauing' and significant improvements are increasingly difficult to secure. It remains the case that social factors are disproportionately significant in their impact on children's academic achievement. It may therefore be an appropriate time to focus on the social environment of the learner rather than increasing the emphasis on the technology of teaching and the dominant hegemony of school improvement.

A number of trends reinforce the increasing emphasis being placed on the relationship between schools and their communities:

1. The increasing evidence of the importance of the social context that schools work in as a critical determinant of educational success.

2. The emergence of clusters and networks as a vehicle of school improvement and innovation.

3. The need to develop understanding of the processes that inform the internal effectiveness of schools as social organizations and so enhance their capacity to support learning.

4. The increasing importance attached to co-operation and collaboration between the agencies that provide services for children and young people.

5. Recognition of the importance of engagement with communities as the basis of a holistic model of education (NCSL, 2004b).

There are three dominant themes to this book: first is the centrality and importance of social capital. Human relationships are fundamental to educational and social development, while learning is a social process; communities only exist to the extent to which they develop the quality of human relationships. The second theme is encapsulated in the concept of moving from 'find and fix' to 'predict and prevent'. Schools traditionally place more emphasis on putting things right rather than stopping them going wrong. This book argues that the most powerful form of prevention in education is a focus on all aspects of the social life of children and young people.

The overarching theme is that education is fundamentally about social justice, equity and inclusion. This book is rooted in the principle that every child and young person has a fundamental entitlement to equal educational opportunities.

We are very grateful to Ingrid Bradbury who has provided invaluable support in the production of this book.

About the authors

John West-Burnham

John West-Burnham is a writer, teacher and consultant in education leadership. He has been a school teacher, teacher trainer and education officer, and has held posts in five universities. John is the author or editor of 19 books and has worked in 20 countries. He is currently honorary professor of education at Queen's University, Belfast and is senior research adviser to the National College for School Leadership.

Maggie Farrar

Maggie Farrar is an operational director at the National College for School Leadership in England. Her early teaching career was in schools in West Africa and London. She was the founding principal of the University of the First Age, a national charity that develops extended learning experiences for young people.

Since May 2003 Maggie has been a director at the National College of School Leadership, where she is responsible for community leadership and the *Every Child Matters* policy area.

George Otero

Dr George Otero is founder and co-president of The Center for RelationaLearning in Santa Fe, New Mexico. In partnership with Susan Chambers-Otero, he established the Centre after successfully operating an educational training centre in Taos, New Mexico, for 20 years.

George Otero is also founder and director of Las Palomas, a non-profit educational centre, started in 1977, devoted to innovative educational programmes for the twenty-first century. He has designed and facilitated over 500 workshops and retreats for business, school, community and youth groups. Creating tailored programmes and workshops on art, culture, history, education, organizational change and cross-cultural communication, he served over 40,000 people and hundreds of diverse organizations since its inception 22 years ago.

Part 1

Education and the community

1 A critique of schools and schooling

Introduction

The work of the three authors of this book and the focus of the series of seminars they have been facilitating in Australia, New Mexico and England, over the last three years, have been driven by a set of questions for which answers are constantly being sought. These questions form the core of this book and are as follow:

1. Do we really believe we are maximizing the achievement of every child?
2. Do we think that schools are doing as well as they could?
3. Do schools have an infinite capacity for improvement?
4. Can the improvement we have seen in school standards over the past decade be extended and enhanced?
5. Can we carry on doing what we have been doing and still manage to meet the needs of those young people who are achieving the least within the current system?
6. Where can we see future practice in the present – what are people doing together to change practice?

The authors chose to use Putnam's (2003) title *Better Together* to base their workshops on, because central to their view of education in the future is the notion of partnership. They regard education as a complex, diffuse process which is the result of the interaction of a wide range of variables, the most significant of which are outside the formal school system. This book is therefore a sustained argument for an integrated approach to a child's education, recognizing the equal rights and responsibilities of all stakeholders – children and young people, their families, the wider community, all the statutory and voluntary agencies, and schools.

This chapter provides the context and rationale for the rest of the book:

- The argument for change
- New approaches to school and community development
- The emerging debate.

The argument for change

This chapter, and indeed this book, will argue that school improvement as we have known it is running out of energy. Schools face a unique set of pressures, both from within the education system and wider society. The 'one size fits all' approach to schooling is being questioned, while at the same time schools are often seen as bulwarks against an increasingly fragmented society.

Peter Senge et al. (2000), in *Schools that Learn*, sum it up when they ask:

> Do we really want to re-create the schools we remember from our own childhoods? Do we want to stop the flow of change and create stagnant pools of schooling because that's what educators were moulded to fit into? (page 10)

They rightly acknowledge that schools learn only at three interdependent levels – the classroom, the school and the community. Senge and his colleagues offer us a challenge – schools that learn only from within are doomed to stagnate. They have to engage with the wider community. This view is reinforced by Gardner (2006):

> Even though it would be optimal if all educational needs could be met within the walls of each school, such comprehensive service is not feasible. Schools can do a good job in covering the traditional curriculum and in developing some of the intelligences, but it is unrealistic to expect them to meet all needs, nourish all intelligences, and to cover all subjects. (page 188)

In many communities, schools represent the biggest single public investment and are the best-resourced organizations – yet many only function for 15 per cent of the year. More importantly, there is a symbiotic link between schools and their communities, and therefore a shared purpose: the nurturing of young lives. Schooling is a necessary, although not sufficient, component of education. Edgar (2001) has given us food for thought when he states:

Today's parents are demanding more ... They want some say in the values and behaviour standards followed by a school, ... They see themselves as partners in the education process and want teacher advice on how they can support their child's learning at home. (page 157)

If this is the case, and the authors believe that it is, then schools need to be successful with their communities, not in spite of them.

This is why improving schools that are single autonomous organizations cannot be sustained indefinitely and will always be finite. One can already observe results at a national level 'plateauing' and school leaders internationally are reporting that significant improvements are increasingly difficult to secure. As always, it remains the case that social factors are disproportionately significant in their impact on children's academic achievement.

As school leaders know, even though learning and teaching is our core business, a child doesn't bring only their brain to school. Looking after the whole child means addressing every aspect of their emotional, physical and educational being – something schools cannot hope to deliver in isolation. (Munby, cited in NCSL, 2006b, page 24)

From the work the three authors have done in three different countries – Australia, the US and England – there appears to be a global shift in our acknowledgement that merely 'improving what is' will not meet the challenge of securing excellence and equity for every child. We see a significant global move towards focusing our attention as educators and as leaders of educational institutions on the broader social environment of the learner, and of engaging with a range of players in that context. For some this is liberation from the current somewhat exclusive emphasis on the technology of teaching and learning within the classroom context; for others it is a challenge. This book is designed to accelerate and support this shift from schooling within a single institution to education across a locality, of which school is one necessary but not exclusive component.

Why are we seeing this shift now?

The first reason for this shift is that the current approach is reaching its natural conclusion; it is quite simply running out of steam. The last decade of the twentieth century was the decade of school improvement. Vast amounts of energy were expended in improving the outcomes of schooling – and they were generally successful. By a range of criteria, schools were much better at schooling: literacy and numeracy scores rose and there was significant improvement against a range of criteria. This was largely achieved through the implementation of national strategies at institutional level. But the gains were not enjoyed by everyone. In England, in particular, there is an education system that is characterized by high excellence – young people are achieving better results than ever but by low equity – the gap between those who achieve and those who do not is getting wider. In other words, in England there is a long tail of chronic underachievement, and no one yet appears to know what to do about it.

The second reason is that the context in which schools operate is changing rapidly. Schools exist in, and are helping to create, a rapidly changing context locally, nationally and globally. Good illustrations of this are the six scenarios for the future of schooling created by the Organization for Economic Co-operation and Development (OECD) first published in *What Schools for the Future?* (2001).

The scenarios are descriptive pictures or stories that help individuals or organizations understand the complexities and uncertainties of their own potential futures. They reflect the national and global trends that we see today, translated into imagined, possible futures. The six scenarios are divided into three areas: 'meltdown' (bureaucratic school systems continue/teacher exodus); reschooling (schools as core social centres/focused learning organizations); and deschooling (learning networks and the learning society/the extension of the market model).

The defining characteristics of each scenario are interesting. The reader will notice that elements of the current system are present in all six. The future is being created here and now.

Bureaucratic school systems continue

This scenario is built on the continuation of powerfully bureaucratic systems, strong pressures towards uniformity and resistance to radical change. Schools are highly distinct institutions, knitted together within complex administrative arrangements. Political and media commentaries are frequently critical in tone but, despite the criticisms, radical change is resisted.

Teacher exodus

In the meltdown scenario there would be a major crisis of teacher shortages, which are highly resistant to conventional policy responses. It is triggered by a rapidly ageing profession, exacerbated by low teacher morale and buoyant opportunities in more attractive graduate jobs. The large size of the teaching force makes improvements in relative attractiveness costly, with long lead times for measures to show tangible results on overall numbers. This has detrimental effects on student learning, particularly in socio-economically disadvantaged communities. A crisis and fortress mentality prevails.

Schools as core social centres

The school as a core social centre enjoys widespread recognition as the most effective bulwark against social, family and community fragmentation. It is now clearly defined by collective and community tasks. This leads to extensive shared responsibilities between schools and other community bodies, sources of expertise, and institutions of further and continuing education, shaping, not conflicting, with high teacher professionalism. The focus of learning is broadened and the curriculum is enriched.

Schools as focused learning organizations

Schools as focused learning organizations are revitalized around a strong knowledge, rather than social agendas, in a culture of high quality, experimentation, diversity and innovation. New forms of evaluation and competence assessment flourish. Information and communication technology (ICT) is used extensively alongside other, traditional and new, learning media. Knowledge management moves to the fore, and the very large majority of schools justifies the label 'learning organization' with extensive links to tertiary education and diverse other organizations. Learning is underpinned by flourishing and interactive research on pedagogy, and the science of learning that is systematically applied.

Learning networks and the learning society

Dissatisfaction with institutionalized provision and expression given to diversified demand leads to the abandonment of schools in favour of a multitude of learning networks, quickened by the extensive possibilities of powerful, inexpensive ICT. The deinstitutionalization, even dismantling, of school systems is part of the emerging 'network society'. Various cultural, religious and community voices come to the fore in the socialization and learning arrangements for children, some very local in character, others using distance and cross-border networking. Community interests, different cultures and personalization are met through small group, home schooling and individualized arrangements for learning.

Extension of the market model

Existing market features in education are significantly extended as governments encourage diversification in a broader environment of market-led change. This is fuelled by the dissatisfaction of 'strategic consumers' in cultures where schooling is commonly viewed as a private, as well as public, good. Many new providers are stimulated to come into the learning market, encouraged by thorough-going reforms of funding structures, incentives and regulations. Innovation abounds, as do painful transitions and inequalities.

It seems clear from this that strategies for improving schools are starting to shift their emphasis, and will not exclusively focus on the school as a single autonomous institution, improving largely from within.

The population explosion in Britain during the nineteenth century is often attributed to improvements in medical science and practice. In fact this only impacted on a minority of the population – the really significant improvements were the result of the provision of clean drinking water and sewerage systems. The change in the death rate and growth of population resulted from the following:

- a focus on sewers not surgeons;
- a shift from the cure to the prevention of disease;
- an investment in a complex infrastructure rather than individual professional technology.

For the public services this means:

- a focus on collaborative effort and locality improvement rather than the professional and the organization;
- a focus on prediction and prevention, rather than finding and fixing;
- a focus on the whole child (learning, well-being and social justice) rather than a narrow focus on the experience within the classroom.

Schools cannot ignore contextual and environmental issues. It is an important factor in educational achievement. While one would not want to present it as an excuse for poor achievement in academic terms, it certainly is an explanation. As Power et al. (2002) conclude in their study:

> ... [educational] outcomes in deprived areas are worse than those in non-deprived areas, whether they are measured in terms of qualification, attendance, exclusions or 'staying on' rates. Inner-city areas in particular feature as having low outcomes. (page 26)

They go on to point out that, in England in the 1990s, 'the gap in outcomes grew rather than narrowed' (page 64). They also point to the need to reduce the 'compositional effects that appear to result from high concentrations of disadvantaged students' (page 65). A significant issue emerges in their conclusion that:

> ... schools serving deprived populations could do more to ensure better home–school relations, which appear to be less facilitative than those in schools serving non-deprived areas. (page 66)

Schools in deprived areas have a great deal in common with schools in non-deprived areas – the same curriculum, assessment regimes, inspection and accountability models, and so on. There are some significant differences in funding, teacher supply and access to resources but these are not broadly consistent as causal factors. What is consistent is the notion of deprivation. The gap is widening not narrowing and there is a growing awareness that we need to act. This is a challenge – and will require a re-conceptualization of the role of schools and education professionals in relation to children, young people, families, communities and other agencies. It will also require a shift in how schools view their communities. From 'the problem is out there', to 'the solution to the problems we face are out there'; in other words, pathologizing communities to seeing them as a rich resource and a collaborator in improvement.

Stephen Meek (2006) recently spoke on social mobility and the attainment gap, and concluded that social factors are the biggest driver of the attainment gap – but that educational levers are also strong. He argues that tackling social factors is critical, but it is harder for governments to effect change in this area, particularly in relation to parental factors.

The authors would argue that this is partly because tackling these factors requires relational learning and personal engagement, which cannot be mandated by policy but can be brokered by schools and communities working together. We will return to relational learning in Chapter 4.

Ruth Kelly, former Secretary of State for Education and Skills, talking at an Institute for Public Policy Research (IPPR) seminar in April 2006, set out the tough questions in the social justice agenda:

- Why is it that, when children start primary school, their readiness to learn remains dependent on who their parents are and where they live?
- Why is it that for so long in this country, at every stage of the school system, many working-class children make less progress than their middle-class counterparts?
- And why is it that too few people leave the education system with the skills they need to get on in life?

The IPPR seminar concluded that place does affect education because of factors such as:

- low aspirations because of history or weak labour markets;
- alternatives to formal education – such as drug dealing, paid labour or crime;
- effects of neighbourhood stigma on self-esteem and learner identity;
- parental isolation and low social capital;
- limited educational resources, library, ICT, play areas, supervised youth activity.

It also concluded that schools are in the best position to help to 'turn this curve' as they are embedded in neighbourhoods to a greater extent than any other public service (Aldridge, 2006).

Studies of schools (Chapman and Harris, 2004), that have begun to shift this link between place, ability and social mobility, have identified the following characteristics of early success:

- a shared belief in the potential for growth and development in all students and staff;
- a distributed leadership approach;
- investment in staff development;
- emphasis on high-quality personal relationships;
- a commitment to the interconnectedness of home, school and community;
- strategies to foster social and emotional development as a precursor to learning.

Similar work by Warren (2005), as part of a Harvard study into urban reform, concludes:

> What sense does it make to try and reform schools while the communities around them stagnate or collapse? Conversely can community building and development efforts succeed in revitalising inner-city neighbourhoods if the public schools within them continue to fail their students? The fates of urban schools and communities are linked, and yet schools reformers and community builders act as if they are not. (page 133)

The study also concluded that community initiatives make a number of critical contributions to schools' improvement, and work best where the school and the community are working together in a constantly improving relationship and context. They can:

- improve the social context so that children come to school better able to learn;
- foster parental and community participation;
- work to transform the predominant culture of the school to one of achievement and equity and hold the school accountable for gains;
- help to build political constituency for better support for schools in disadvantaged neighbourhoods.

In other words, engaged and demanding parents and communities help to improve schools, while engaged and demanding schools help to improve communities. This is an area that will be returned to in Chapter 5 when the role of parents is looked at.

In England these findings influenced work on the revision of the *National Standards for Headteachers* (DfES, 2004). A new standard, 'Strengthening community through collaboration', was introduced, which recognizes the interdependent nature of school and community. This standard states that:

> Schools exist in a distinctive social context which has a direct impact on what happens outside school. School leadership should commit to engaging with the internal and external school community to secure equity and entitlement. Headteachers collaborate with other schools in order to bring positive benefits to their own and each other's schools.

Headteachers should work collaboratively at both strategic and operational levels with parents and carers and across multiple agencies for the well being of all children. Headteachers should be aware that school improvement and community development are interdependent and that they share responsibility with others for the leadership of the wider educational system. (DfES, 2004, page 11)

When the first headteachers' standards were developed in 1996, this understanding of school and community interdependence was not apparent. The standards focused exclusively on improving and leading the school from within. The NCSL sees this shift as heralding a 'renaissance for leaders' who are committed to following a course of transformation in schools that is underpinned by a moral and social justice agenda, and which, for many, is the reason they came into teaching as a profession (NCSL, 2006b). For once the policy context is in alignment with the shifts at local level and the challenge appears to be shared.

Perhaps David Miliband, then Minister for School Standards, summed up the challenge in 2003 when he said at the North of England Education Conference:

Where you are born and the family you are born into still has a strong effect on your life chances. The key factors are poverty, family circumstances, the neighbourhood you live in and the school you go to.

Miliband said this about England and it led to one of the most significant changes in living memory designed to transform the lives of children and protect the most vulnerable: *Every Child Matters* (HM Government, 2003). It is designed to shift the focus from dealing with the consequences of difficulties in children's lives to preventing things going wrong in the first place. It equally applies to all children, whoever they are and wherever they live. It also aims to promote professional respect and trust between agencies, and ensure that collaboration works well:

For schools, it places a greater focus on the promotion of activity which many school leaders already embrace; extended services in and around school, multi agency working and the development of children's centres. It also creates a drive towards new and more authentic relationships between schools and parents, families, children, young people and the whole community to ensure that the services on offer are wanted and targeted at those who need them. (NCSL, 2006b, page 6)

This radical reform was introduced in 2003 with the following statement:

This is the beginning of a long journey which will present challenges for all of us, but from which we must not flinch. We will be called upon to make common cause across professional boundaries and with reformed structures and services to create the means by which the needs, interests and welfare of children can be better protected and advanced. Children are precious. They are entitled not just to the sentiment of adults but a strategy that safeguards them as children and realises their potential to the very best of our ability. (DfES, 2003, page 4)

This connection between standards, well-being and social equity is echoed throughout a whole 'tableau' of policies, public sector reform initiatives and international studies, all designed to secure social justice. For the first time schools have a mandate to 'think' and 'do' differently:

- *Personalization* – opening up learning and personalizing the offer within and beyond school.
- *The PISA* (Programme for International Student Assessment) *study* – addressing the problem that won't go away – the UK has a system characterized by high excellence but low equity.
- *Schools working together* – the development of networks, federations, clusters and confederations.
- *The development of new professionals* – remodelling integrated professional services for children.
- *Schools as public spaces* – a shift in ownership.
- *Public sector reform and the customer* – empowering the customer to demand high quality and help in the improvement of the service.
- *The importance of the local* – the generation of local solutions to national issues.

The last two points are probably the most significant in relation to the challenges we are exploring in this book. Government policies and their means of development and delivery, to date, fail to address the issues of accountability, motivation and uniqueness at a local and personal level – issues of 'personal accountability, internal motivation and uniqueness'. Rather they emphasize consistency, conformity and compliance. Geoff Mulgan (2000) commented on this when, looking back at the first term of the Labour government, he concluded:

> Too much was imposed top-down rather than involving communities themselves; too many initiatives were short-term; too many focused on one or two problems rather than tackling the cluster of related problems in the round. (page 184)

For Mulgan, two of the key themes in the newly 'emerging agenda' for learning are:

- Policies for knowledge that go wider than formal education: diet, housing and poverty bear directly on cognitive development and educational performance.
- .... And as a result education and learning will increasingly take place beyond educational institutions … (pages 151–152)

New approaches to school and community development

School improvement reinforces the school as a closed system, whereas, in order to continue to raise standards and ensure that all children have the potential and the support they need to achieve, they must begin to act much more as open systems.

Because schools have claimed sole responsibility for educational provision, they have found themselves at odds and often out of touch with the educational aspirations of the society of which they are a part. Schools, like other institutions, find themselves operating as silos: out of touch and no longer an integral part of the community. Given this reality, schools cannot only be about the business of improving themselves; they also need to address this isolation and alienation. Schools must transform their relationship with the community. This involves changing attitudes, relationships and the deployment of resources.

Schools are living human systems and as such survive, develop and transform by experiencing, owning and integrating differences. This is accomplished by bringing together a diverse set of stakeholders to discover common ground through a democratic process, thereby developing social capital and reconnecting schools and communities. The process that is best known for building educational capacity in a community and has demonstrated success worldwide is called a future search.

Developed over 20 years by Weisbord and Janoff (2000), the future search is an action guide to finding common ground in organizations and communities. As a process that builds capacity across diverse communities, it is unmatched in developing social capital and collaborative working relationships among the diverse constituents that make up contemporary school communities. As Weisbord and Janoff state in their preface:

> In future search people have a chance to take down the walls and assume more control of their future. Many participants welcome the chance to take responsibility and to learn and work with people from other walks of life. People are always more secure knowing first hand where others stand, and may begin in this setting to accept differences – in background, viewpoints, and values – as realities to be lived with, not problems to be solved. (page 10)

Bolton future search case study

As in many local authorities, for Bolton, in north-west England, communication and information sharing are key issues between services whose sector boundaries are keenly observed.

There is needless duplication. One head describes attending a meeting to discuss the welfare of a family of six children where five headteachers, three social workers and four health workers attended, all with different perspectives. Funding anomalies means cash is strictly earmarked 'education', 'social services' or 'health', and tapping into someone else's pot appears to be strictly forbidden.

To tackle some of these structural and cultural barriers, Ingrid Cox, deputy head at Rivington and Blackrod High School and co-leader of the Bolton pastoral network learning community, working with Bolton Metropolitan Borough Council, organized a 'Future Search' workshop, which saw school leaders and others from education join representatives from the social care, local authority, police, charity and voluntary sectors to generate a shared agenda and talk about the changes needed to ensure that 'every child matters' in their area.

By the end of the final day, everyone in the room approved each group's core values and action plans. What was not agreed was written as 'not agreed'. People committed to their own actions. On the final day, each group produced statements on their chosen theme for improvement.

It was all the more powerful because most of the people in the room had never worked together before. Uniquely, children – some still at primary school – attended the stakeholder event and throughout the process worked on an equal footing with adult representatives.

The authority is now planning to put together a framework for children's and young people's priorities, and to set up a young people's forum to continue to gather views and ideas from young people about the services they want and need.

The Bolton Local Authority team has also 'torn up' the work they had started on models of delivery for *Every Child Matters* in the light of what they have gleaned from working with other stakeholders at the Future Search event. They now see the need to work beyond the statutory sector to enable *Every Child Matters* to be realized (NCSL, 2005c).

A blog was set up following the event, which students have responded to energetically – a particular blog from one of the students, Naeem, captures in its last sentence the essence of collaborative engagement for improvement between all living and working in a locality.

Day 3: Naeem's notions

Bolton's Future Search is over ... but the real work has just begun! It's totally down to us whether or not we will make Every Child Matter in Bolton ... or we will have attended this event and made empty promises. I have great faith in everyone who came to the conference and I'm sure great things will come of it.

These three brilliant days will live with me forever, and I hope this blog will also live for years to come ... this can be a great place to post updates about what you've been up to and use it to communicate with other stakeholders.

It wouldn't work without me, it wouldn't without you, but it has the potential to be great if we work together. (www.boltonfuturesearch.blogspot.com)

George Green's community audit case study: 'The writing on the wall'

George Green's School is a large comprehensive school in the London Borough of Tower Hamlets.

In 2004 the school wanted to enhance its already strong child-centred ethos and become even more outcome driven. The staff were keen to develop the school as one that is 'permeable' and learns and improves through full engagement with the local community. They were aware that as a full service community school they could already be limiting the resources available to them by thinking too narrowly. They wanted to begin this journey by drawing on accurate information on what people wanted and valued from the school. They embarked on a community audit, facilitated by Rezolv and commissioned by George Green's School and the NCSL. They wanted to engage with a process which:

- built leadership capacity within the school as a community;
- established broad and equal participation with the local community;
- secured a shared commitment for change from everyone;
- created a collaborative culture for future work.

This consisted of a series of 'open space' activities around three questions displayed on three large walls:

1. What does every child need?
2. What do we already have in our community for children?
3. What do children need at each stage of their development?

Different coloured Post-its designated different groups and allowed the thoughts of 362 individuals to be recorded. Some of the key findings were:

- The relative emphasis on different issues varies. Homework was emphasized by parents and students but not teachers. Holiday activities were emphasized more by parents than students. Space and environment were more important to students than parents and teachers.
- The way professionals perceive the school and the local community from the outside differs from how students and local people perceive it from the inside. In particular, parents and students tend to limit their understanding of what is possible by their experience of current services.
- The awareness of resources beyond professional domains that could be mobilized. Some of the envisaged entitlements could be met by growing community resources, rather than professional provision.
- The vastness of the resource and the need for tangible commitment.

> No table is big enough to seat the people required to deliver the entitlement envisaged by the 'writing on the wall' activity. First steps must be to establish a zeal for the table and allow for early exit if it is found wanting. A partner (including the school) delivering tangible commitment is more meaningful than one nodding to partnership rhetoric. (Rezolv, 2004, page 13)

Winsford case study

Winsford is a town in Cheshire that experiences significant social and economic disadvantage within a relatively affluent county. There are 17 schools in Winsford and they have all benefited from a recent single regeneration budget (SRB) project which has aimed to improve basic skills across the town. In addition, they are all part of the 'Winsford by Choice' initiative and form the 'Winsford Education Partnership'. Early discussion in Winsford focused on key areas of work and key questions they wanted to address:

Key themes and areas of work were:

- Creating a shared understanding of 'leadership' and 'community'.
- Understand more about what is happening now – what do the community value?
- How will we enable the whole community to engage in the design of 'what now for Winsford?'?

Questions/issues

- Do we know who the community feel are the highly effective agencies and individuals in meeting their needs – are they part of this strategy?
- How will this shift the power relationship – what are the implications for individuals and organizations?
- Are we all clear about what we want – where is our own self-interest in this and how do we recognize and declare it?

As a result of this initial work, in 2004 Winsford held its third whole-town training and development day. Four hundred and fifty people attended from schools, organizations and the community – including town residents and children. They used a card game (web link to it – freely available on www.ncsl.org.uk/mediastore/image2/nlg-wawla3-8-creating-community-links.pdf).

As a result, the town agreed that it had an overwhelming reason to work together. It was phrased as:

> Schools and communities should be more closely linked so that children's self esteem will be improved and aspirations can be raised. Schools and other agencies can work together to

'break the cycle' and lose the negative image of the town. By doing this we hope that we can bring education back to the child where it rightfully belongs. (NCSL, 2005b, page 3)

For each of the past three summers, Winsford has held an arts festival. In 2006 this was on the theme of 'Winsford wishes'. Children wrote their wishes on paper raindrops – and a waterfall of rainbows was displayed at Asda supermarket and in books lodged at the Winsford library to provide a permanent record of 3,346 wishes. This is a powerful reminder of what is possible and a valuable resource for decision makers in the town of Winsford.

The emerging debate

From the work the authors have done, it appears that embracing school and community improvement as an interdependent strategy is a complex but necessary endeavour if schools are not going to become 'beached' in a twentieth-century model. Improving an institution is specific, focused and controllable; improving an institution within a community is diffuse and complex. But schools are well placed to embrace this shift. Schools, as we shall see in Chapter 4, are institutions that tend to have unusually high levels of social capital. Educational leadership is fundamentally concerned with values and is essentially aspirational in nature. Schools as organizations have a strong moral purpose.

But it would be wrong to pretend that such a change is going to be easy. Building capacity in communities for this next stage of improvement will require a range of qualities and strategies that are implicit to running schools but which need a different approach as they shift to promote full engagement with the community.

These qualities and strategies, as listed below, will be explored further in this book:

1. A vision for the community based on consensual values and aspirations.
2. Building capacity through dialogue, conversations and engagement.
3. Highly developed relational skills rooted in trust and respect.
4. A commitment to democratic processes.
5. The ability to work with networks.
6. A commitment to shared learning through experience.

The key messages in this initial chapter are those that have engaged educators over the last two years of the Better Together series of seminars. Participants in those seminars have summarized these key messages and have identified their own personal learning.

In reflecting on this chapter, look at these messages and ask how far your learning, at this point, accords with theirs.

Better Together – key messages

School improvement has had a demonstrable impact on standards to date:

- The improvement cannot be sustained indefinitely and we are already aware of the plateau effect in Key Stage results.
- Social factors are disproportionately significant in their impact on children's achievement.
- Community leadership works to achieve better outcomes in three domains – social justice, well-being and standards.
- School improvement leads to institutional bonding. A further improvement in standards, achievement and satisfaction will come about through organizations bridging with one another and with other agencies and community groups.
- The development of 'relational trust' between the school, community and other agencies is a prerequisite of better partnerships leading to better outcomes and sustainable improvement.
- Better partnerships and trust in communities are developed through the promotion and practice of dialogue.
- Developing the skills of dialogue takes time and practice.

The focus on standards has meant a lesser focus on social justice and well-being; this has exacerbated, not alleviated, the equity gap in standards and has limited the potential of schools to improve:

- School – community collective transformation and improvement requires schools and school leaders to practise 'power with', not 'power over'.
- This requires a reorientation of the role of schools within a community, in other words they are a necessary but not sufficient contributor to the learning of young people.
- There is an implied extension of focus from 'teachers in schools' to 'educators across the community'.
- There is a need to introduce greater community-based governance and accountability for learning in a local area.
- The current extended school policy could lead to larger and more powerful schools with little real community engagement; however, the policy is young enough for this to be addressed.
- A much more sophisticated understanding of the links between social, intellectual and organizational capital in communities is required if we are to draw on all three in our quest for improvement of place and organizations.

2 The social context of education

Chapter 1 has demonstrated what might be described as a crisis in schooling. It can be described as a crisis because traditional strategies and remedies are clearly not working – the challenging goal of reconciling equity and excellence across the education system remains elusive. Indeed, there seems to be an impasse, if not an actual deterioration, in terms of performance across the system. This is not to deny the remarkable achievements of individual schools and local authorities but to point to the continuing polarization in terms of access to educational achievement.

The prevailing orthodoxy for a generation has been to focus on improving schools. School improvement has emerged as the dominant hegemony but it has always been recognized that its related policies and strategies can only address a small proportion of the factors that influence the achievement and life chances of children and young people.

> Most school effectiveness studies show that 80% or more of student achievement can be explained by student background rather than schools. (Silins and Mulford, 2002, page 561)

Rutter and his colleagues (1979) found that 'schools do make a difference' but recognized that this was in terms of attendance, behaviour and attainment – in essence, students perform better in schools that are effective social institutions, in other words some schools are better at being schools than others. This is important because it provides a very clear model of what the most controllable of the variables influencing a young person's life chances should look like:

> … our investigation clearly showed that secondary schools varied markedly with respect to their pupils' behaviour, attendance, exam success and delinquency…This suggests that, contrary to many views, secondary schools do have an important influence on their pupils' behaviour and attainments. (Rutter et al., 1979, page 205)

This highlights a key issue in the school improvement movement – the differences (or variations) between schools. If 80 per cent of student achievement is explained by student background and then only 20 per cent is attributable to the school, then schools show a wide range of effectiveness. The authors' argument is that much of the energy, resource and intellectual investment has focused on the 20 per cent and has ignored the 80 per cent. This is not to deny the importance of ensuring that the school is as effective as possible.

Figure 2.1 offers a model of the variables that will influence a child's educational success and life chances.

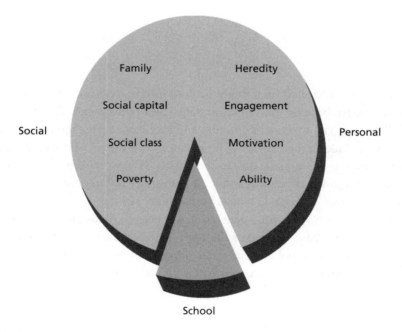

Figure 2.1 The variables influencing a child's life chances

No significance should be attached to the relative positioning of the variables – they will be in multiple permutations according to the individual. The key point of the figure is that the school is less significant than the social and personal factors are. Desforges (2003) provides graphic illustrations of the relative impact of schools and social factors:

> ... a great deal of the variation in students' achievement is outside the school's influence. Family social class, for example, accounts for about one third of such variance. (page 21)

> ... parental involvement in the form of 'at-home' interest and support is a major force in shaping pupils' educational outcomes. (page 22)

The rest of this chapter is devoted to an analysis of the social factors on the educational success and life chances of children and young people. Although the personal factors are not a direct concern of this book, it is worth noting that the increasing focus on learning and approaches to personalizing educational experiences recognize the need to address this area as much as the social aspects.

The four social factors influencing educational success or failure are: the quality of family life, the level of wealth or poverty, the level of social capital in the community and the social class of the family. When these factors are all positive, then schooling will tend to work and personal and social success are much more likely. However, if the factors are negative, then success is far less likely and dysfunctionality is probable.

The relationship between these four elements is demonstrated in Figure 2.2. The presence of any one of the four is likely to compromise educational and personal success; a combination of any of these factors renders personal success increasingly problematic.

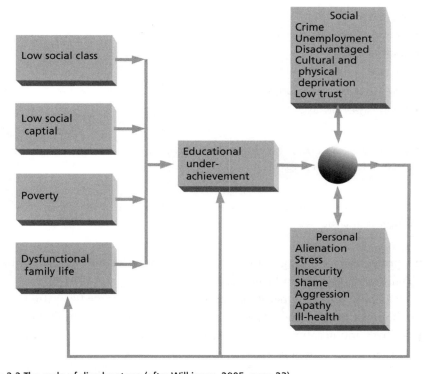

Figure 2.2 The cycle of disadvantage (after Wilkinson, 2005, page 23)

A diagram such as Figure 2.2 inevitably over-simplifies very complex relationships and creates a possibly false determinism. It is important to stress that there is not an automatic causality – there are intervening variables and this is not a form of predestination, as Wilkinson (2005) points out:

> As everything in the social world affects everything else, every box in the diagram could be linked with bidirectional arrows to every other. The figure is an attempt to suggest the causal processes that lead from greater material inequality, on the left-hand side, to various psychological, behavioral, and health outcomes, on the right. (page 24)

The government's report, *Every Child Matters* (HM Government, 2003) does establish a direct link between the factors shaping children's life chances:

> Although research has not built up a detailed picture of the causal links, certain factors are associated with poor outcomes including:
>
> - low income and parental unemployment
> - homelessness
> - poor parenting
> - poor schooling
> - post-natal depression among mothers
> - low birth weight
> - substance misuse
> - individual characteristics such as intelligence
> - community factors. (page 17)

> The more risk factors a child experiences … the more likely it is they will experience further negative outcomes. (page 18)

> Although experience during the early years is important, life chances continue to be forged throughout children's lives. (page 20)

Every professional working with children and young people will recognize the, almost fatalistic, imperatives in Figure 2.3.

Of course there will be numerous permutations between these two extremes. What is clear in both the positive and negative situations is that there is a multiplier effect at work – positives and negatives are reinforced exponentially. This view is reinforced by the OECD PISA (2001) studies:

> In three other countries – Australia, Belgium and the United Kingdom – high quality of performance is combined with above-average *inequality* in student performance between different socio-economic groups. (page 191)

High social class + relative wealth + positive parenting + high social capital = enhanced life chances

Low social class + poverty + poor parenting + low social capital = diminished life chances

Figure 2.3 The life chances equations

The overall conclusion of this aspect of the PISA study confirms the absolute relationship between social context and personal, social and educational outcomes:

> National research evidence from various countries has generally been discouraging. Schools have appeared to make little difference. Either because privileged families are better able to reinforce and enhance the effect of schools, or because schools are better able to nurture and develop young people from privileged background, it has often been apparent that schools reproduce existing patterns of privilege rather than delivering equal opportunities in a way that can distribute outcomes more equitably. (page 210)

The evidence raises questions about the very nature of schools and this issue is dealt with in detail in Chapter 3. What is clear is that schools, in essence, replicate and reinforce their social context. If there is a commitment to raising academic attainment, educational outcomes and enhancing life chances, then schools may not be the appropriate vehicle. It becomes necessary to engage with the superordinate factors – social class, poverty, family life and social capital. The following sections will consider each of these topics in turn to explore the implications they have for achieving social equity.

Social class

The history of education in Great Britain (particularly England) is absolutely linked to the history of social class. In many ways social class remains the prime determinant of the type of educational experience available to a child or young person. There is a direct and explicit correlation between social class, educational success and life chances. Although the relative ratios may have changed (for example the increase in numbers going on to higher education) social class remains a key determinant of access and success.

It seems strange to return to a discussion on social class after an era in which the 'classless society' was much trumpeted and in which the historic privileges of the upper classes become generally available and the fashion and styles of the lower classes became generally acceptable. As Mount (2004) puts it:

> Surely the freedoms, opportunities and material comfort and security open to the worst-off in this country are immeasurably superior to those enjoyed by people in previous generations who found themselves at the bottom of the heap. We are the beneficiaries of a century and a half of social reform, are we not? (page 14)

In spite of all the changes, social class remains a key determinant of life chances. It remains a fact that members of the upper classes enjoy significant advantages. Members of the higher social classes are more likely to:

- live longer;
- be less subject to illness and make better recoveries when they do fall ill;
- secure educational success;
- secure high status employment;
- own high-quality housing;
- be less subject to crime;
- live in effective communities;
- have healthy diets;
- enjoy a more diverse quality of life;
- access power, influence and status.

For each of the above, the lower classes are likely to experience a negative corollary. This has produced a situation characterized by Hutton (1995) in the following terms:

> For what binds together the disorders of the British system is a fundamental amorality. It is amoral to run a society founded on the exclusion of so many people from decent living standards and opportunities.
>
> These exclusions, while beneficial in the short-term to those inside the circle of privilege, are in the long run inefficient and ultimately undermine the wealth-generating process. (page 24)

This polarization of society is reflected in the education system of England. According to Marmot (2005):

> In fact among all the influences on children's educational performance, the school may not be the most important.
>
> In fact, the league tables for school performance are a remarkably good indicator of the area in which the school is located. The more deprived the area the worse the average

school performance. If you look up a school to see how it is performing, you are actually reading off an exquisitely sensitive indicator of deprivation. (page 225)

Perhaps the most significant exemplification of the power of social class is to be found in the influence of the independent schools sector. Just 7 per cent of young people attend such schools yet, according to a review of research carried out by The Sutton Trust in the *Independent* newspaper (2005), they dominate the professions:

Judges	76%
Barristers	68%
Solicitors	55%
MPs	32%
Front benchers	42%
Life peers	56%
Top journalists	56%
Leaders of FTSE-100 companies	31%

The research also found that 87 per cent of medical students come from managerial or professional backgrounds. The Russell Group of 19 leading universities recruited 73 per cent of their intake from the three highest social groups. There appears to be evidence that the upper classes are strengthening their hold on the professions – in fact the polarization of society is increasing in every respect. In 1991 the proportion of the nation's wealth owned by the top 1 per cent was 17 per cent; in 2002 it was 23 per cent.

Sir Peter Lampl (in Power et al., 2006) summaries the situation thus:

> Year after year the list of the hundred highest-ranking schools in England is dominated by independent schools which, according to a comparative analysis by the OECD, are the best performing schools in the world. The corollary of this success, however, is that the UK has the largest performance gap between the independent and state sectors of any country in the world, which means that 7% of children in fee-paying schools have a significant advantage over their less affluent peers in maintained schools, taking a disproportionate number of places at our top universities and in our highly-paid professions. (page 3)

Social class has a huge impact on educational achievement and on individuals' life chances. It is impact based on relative wealth, perceived privilege and a wide range of cultural factors centred on expectations, aspiration, social confidence, networks and a shared commitment to preserving an elite status based on hierarchy. It totally compromises any notions of equity or equality in British society.

Poverty

Social class is almost invariably related to wealth – although occasionally there are stories of members of the upper classes bravely coping with genteel poverty. Britain has one of the highest levels of child poverty in the developed world – in Europe only Portugal, Italy, Ireland and Spain have higher levels. There is an absolute, consistent and persistent correlation between child poverty and social and educational failure. It is not intended to enter the academic debate about the nature of poverty – in essence, poverty will always be a relative concept. The following data are taken from the House of Commons Work and Pensions Committee Report (2004) *Child Poverty in the UK* and provides the quantitative basis for this section:

Following substantial growth in the national child poverty rate from the early 1980s, the rate peaked at around 34% in 1996–97 and since then has been on a downward trend. Currently, some 3.6 million children in Great Britain are in relative poverty – a rate of 28% ... (page 13)

The proportion of workless households doubled from less than 10% in the mid 1970s to nearly 20% in 1996 – the rate is currently just under 16%, and for households with children in 15%. (page 13)

The child poverty rate is also affected by the large-scale changes in family formation that have occurred in recent decades with a large increase in lone parent families, who now make up a quarter of all families with children in the UK. The proportion of children living in lone parent families increased from 7% in 1972 to 25% in 2003. (page 13)

The children of teenage parents are more likely than children of older parents to be in poverty and are also more likely to suffer adverse outcomes as they get older. In addition, the likelihood of teenage pregnancy is greater for those who have grown up in poverty. (page 14)

Other instances of social change have occurred which are also strongly associated with poverty. These include an increase in rates of people reporting a limiting long-term illness or disability, an increasing minority ethnic population and an increase in people seeking asylum in the UK. (page 14)

26% of white children lived in income poverty compared with 75% of Pakistani/Bangladeshi children, 53% of black non-Caribbean, 39% of black Caribbean children and 22% of Indian children. (page 18)

Child poverty varies substantially across different geographical areas of the UK too. At a country level, the HBAI [households below average income] statistics show that child poverty in Wales was slightly higher (30% compared to 29% in England and 27% in both Scotland and Northern Ireland). Using a different poverty measure recent research on poverty in Northern Ireland found that the child poverty rate in Northern Ireland was 37% compared to 30% in Great Britain. At a regional level, London has the highest child poverty rate in Britain (38% for Greater London – rising to 54% in inner London). Other regions in Britain with child poverty rates above the national average of 28% are the North East (37%), Yorkshire and the Humber and North West and Merseyside (both at 30%), and the West Midlands (29%). The lowest child poverty rates were in the South East with a child poverty rate of 20%. (page 19)

It is very difficult to be absolutely confident about the total impact of child poverty but the Economic and Social Research Council (ESRC) Research Briefing (2000) provides some clear indications:

1. *Is there evidence that the outcomes for all children got worse in the last 20 years?*

   Yes for:

   low birth weight, some infections, homelessness, school exclusions, crime, smoking for girls, alcohol, drugs, suicide in young men.

   No for:

   mortality, dental health, fatal accidents, teenage pregnancy, poor housing, educational achievement.

2. *Is there clear evidence that worse outcomes are associated with relative child poverty in the UK?*

   Yes for:

   mortality, most morbidity, fatal accidents, neglect and physical abuse, teenage pregnancy, poor housing, homelessness, educational attainment, smoking, suicide and self-esteem.

   No for:

   crime, sexual abuse, alcohol, drugs, child labour and unhappiness.

3. *Have poor children fared worse than children who are not poor over the last 20 years?*

   Here the evidence gets particularly difficult to interpret but the judgements are:

   Yes for:

   child mortality, low birth weight, accidents, teenage pregnancy, bad housing conditions, educational attainment and suicide.

   No for:

   infant mortality, chronic illness, alcohol, drugs and child labour.

An accessible, and generally reliable, indicator of the relationship between child poverty and educational achievement is the level of free school meals. According to Woodward (2003) the correlation is stark:

In the 100 schools with the highest percentage of pupils on free school meals, 29% of students gain five Cs at GCSE or better – just over half of the 50% national average ... (page 3)

The same schools have 31.9% of pupils with special educational needs, well above the 19.6% national average. And nearly a fifth – 18% – are in debt, at levels averaging £213,000 a school. (page 3)

The top 200 state schools, in terms of GCSE performance, have an average of 3 per cent of students receiving free school meals. This compares with a national average of 14.3 per cent. Significantly, the postcode sectors in which the 200 schools are situated have a free school meal eligibility of 12.3 per cent. Almost two-thirds of the top 200 schools have free school meal rates of less than 2 per cent. In effect, as The Sutton Trust Report (2005) makes clear:

... poorer children are much less likely to benefit from a top quality state education than their better off peers, even if a leading maintained school is on their doorstep. (page 8)

As might be expected, a similar situation applies in primary schools, as shown in Table 2.1.

Table 2.1 Inspection grades by free school meal benchmarks for primary schools

Type of school	Inspection grades	Very good	Good	Some improvement needed	Substantial improvement needed
All schools	Standards achieved by pupils	11	44	40	5
	Quality of education	18	60	21	1
	The school's climate	52	41	6	0
	Management and efficiency	38	43	16	2
Up to and including 8%	Standards achieved by pupils	19	56	23	1
	Quality of education	23	60	16	0
	The school's climate	70	27	2	0
	Management and efficiency	44	41	13	1
More than 50%	Standards achieved by pupils	1	14	66	19
	Quality of education	11	59	27	2
	The school's climate	22	63	13	2
	Management and efficiency	32	48	16	3

Source: adapted from Ofsted (2003, page 26)

What is clear from this table is that in schools with over 50 per cent of free school meals only 15 per cent were classified as very good or good in respect of standards achieved by pupils. In schools with up to 8 per cent of free school meals the figure was 75 per cent. The column indicating substantial improvement required is substantially higher for schools with over 50 per cent free school meals than those with up to 8 per cent. Most tellingly, even when management and efficiency are very good or good in schools with over 50 per cent, standards still require some or substantial improvement in 85 per cent of these schools.

In both primary and secondary examples, it does appear that poverty is a critical variable in determining a school's relative success. The best advice to parents concerned with securing their children's academic success is, do not be poor. However, the figures do show that some children living in poverty do experience academic success.

Family life

It is reasonably possible to be objective about social class (even though there are many cultural and anthropological factors that defy classification) and the definition of poverty (although contentious) is fundamentally empirical. Understanding the family is far more complex and challenging – not least because it is an emotive and value-laden concept.

There is in the British psyche an archetype of the family which, like most archetypes, probably never existed. It centres on the nuclear family with easy access to an extended family – notably grandparents. This model was found in the classics of children's literature and is still found in the ideal world of the advertising agency. It hardly needs adding that such families are invariably middle class with fathers working, mothers at home, holidays by the sea, a dog called Rover and a cat called Tiddles. Such is the power of the archetype that almost any arrangement that does not conform to these criteria is seen as 'deviant' or at best a compromise.

In fact, the concept of family now covers a wide range of permutations which are the result of a range of factors:

- The rise in divorce and remarriage, resulting in what might be called 'step-families'.
- Both parents working and having careers.
- The growth in births to single mothers (40 per cent in 2005).
- Increased mobility, ending the geographically proximate extended family.
- Children having to care for aged, disabled or incapacitated parents.

As Cleaver (2006) summaries it:

> As a result of [these] historical, legal and economic factors, the structure of the family in British society underwent fundamental changes during the twentieth century. Individual children in Britain today will grow up in very different family units – at one extreme a child may live with both his or her birth parents and siblings from the same union. At the other, a child may live with parents neither of whom is related to him or her by blood (for example a stepmother and her new partner) and other children who may be related in a variety of different ways. Along this continuum is a great variety of different types of family unit: one-parent, or step-parent families, both parents and grandparents, or other relatives, or less common constellations such as same sex partners caring for children. (pages 124–125)

Whatever the particular construct there is no doubt that the family is pivotal to educational success and life chances:

> … the family, in whatever form, is the foundation for every child's human capital; it is the crucible of competence. It is also the starting point for every child's networks, its connections with the wider world, its sense of trust of and reciprocal obligations towards 'strangers' in the society as a whole. Married or not, single parent or two, first family or step, based on blood ties, adoption or simply deep friendship, families are the key mediation point between individual and society, the private self and the public self as employee, voter or community group member. (Edgar, 2001, page 31)

Desforges (2003) in his authoritative and definitive review of the research relating to families and education is unambiguous:

> What parents do with their children at home through the age range, is much more significant than any other factor open to educational influence. (page 91)

He is equally robust about the relative significance of the family:

> Research also establishes that parental involvement has a significant effect on children's achievement and adjustment even after all other factors (such as social class, maternal education and poverty) have been take(n) out of the equation between children's aptitudes and their achievement. Differences in parental involvement have a much bigger impact on achievement than differences associated with the effects of school in the primary age range. Parental involvement continues to have a significant effect through the age range although the impact for older children becomes more evident in staying on rates and educational aspirations than as measured achievement. (page 86)

Desforges identifies the factors that determine the level and extent of parental involvement:

- strongly related to family social class: the higher the class the more the involvement;
- strongly related to the level of mothers' education: the higher the level of maternal educational qualification the greater the extent of involvement;
- diminished by material deprivation, maternal psychosocial ill health, and single-parent status;
- diminishes and changes form as the children get older;
- strongly influenced by the child's attainment: the greater the attainment, the greater the degree of involvement;
- strongly influenced by the child: children take a very active role in mediating between parents and schools;
- influenced to some degree by the ethnic culture of the family. (pages 85–86)

Social capital

In many ways social capital is the factor that integrates the various influences on the success and the life chances of children and young people discussed so far in this chapter. Putnam (2000) is unequivocal in his argument about the importance of social capital:

> … child development is powerfully shaped by social capital … trust, networks, and norms of reciprocity within a child's family, school, peer group, and larger community have wide-ranging effects on the child's opportunities and choices and, hence, on behaviour and development. (page 296)

and

> … social capital is second only to poverty in the breadth and depth of its effects on children's lives. (page 296)

Field (2003) is equally robust:

> … the connection between human capital and social capital has rightly been described as 'one of the most robust empirical regularities in the social capital literature' (Glaeser et al., 2002: 455). Even if we do not yet fully understand this pattern, we can conclude with some confidence that there is a close relationship between people's social networks and their educational performance. (page 50)

Social capital is an elusive and contentious concept, fiercely debated by academics yet intuitive common sense to most people. Perhaps the best definition was provided by the philosopher Arthur Schopenhauer as quoted by Buonfino and Mulgan (2006):

> On a cold winter's day, a group of porcupines huddled together to stay warm and keep from freezing. But, soon, they felt one another's quills and moved apart. When the need for warmth brought them closer together again, their quills again forced them apart. They were driven back and forth at the mercy of their discomforts until they found the distance from one another that provided both a maximum of warmth and a minimum of pain. (page 1)

Social capital is essentially about maximizing warmth and minimizing pain – finding the best way to be together. Where there is maximum comfort and minimum pain we flourish and so do the communities we live in:

> The reason why social capital has been attracting attention is because it brings enormous tangible benefits to society. Researchers have been uncovering more and more evidence of links between social capital and desirable outcomes in terms of economic growth, crime, health and education. Among other things, citizens with good networks of relationships have fewer mental problems, recover faster from illness, smoke less and live longer. They are also less likely to commit crime or to be the victim of crime. A society rich in social capital should therefore be better off in many ways, not least because it should need to spend less money on hospitals, prisons and antidepressant drugs. (Martin, 2005, page 87)

Social capital might be best defined by identifying the component elements:

- Shared social norms and values: a clear consensus about the moral basis of the community, principles are known, shared, understood and acted on – they inform community and personal decisions.
- Sophisticated social networks: clear and rich lines of communication with shared language, a common vocabulary and high-quality dialogue.
- High levels of trust: openness, consistency and reliability.
- High civic engagement: people are good citizens; they vote, stand for election and participate in the civic community.
- Symbols and rituals: the community has a sense of identity which is celebrated through shared ceremonies and events.
- Interdependence and reciprocity: there is a high level of caring and sharing, people 'look out for each other'.
- Volunteering and community action: people join in; clubs, societies and charities feature prominently in community action.

Perhaps the most lyrical account of the nature of social capital is provided by Archbishop Desmond Tutu in his definition of *Ubuntu*. *Ubuntu* is a Southern African concept which best translates as 'I am because we are' or 'a person is a person through other people':

> Ubuntu refers to the person who is welcoming, who is hospitable, who is warm and generous, who is affirming of others, who does not feel threatened that others are able and good [this person] has a proper self-assurance that comes from knowing they belong in a greater whole, and know that they are diminished when another is humiliated, is diminished, is tortured, is oppressed, is treated as if they were less than who they are. (Battle, 1997, page 35)

> We say a person is a person through other persons. We don't come fully formed into the world. We learn how to think, how to walk, how to speak, how to behave, indeed how to be human from other human beings. We need other human beings in order to be human. We are made for togetherness, we are made for family, for fellowship, to exist in a tender network of interdependence. ... This is how you have Ubuntu – you care, you are hospitable, you're gentle, you're compassionate and concerned. (Battle, 1997, page 65)

High social capital will explain the success of many different types of community – villages, neighbourhoods, faith communities, orchestras, sports teams, military units and schools. Schools with high social capital may have a significant advantage – this might explain the success of many independent and church schools – they have a ready-made sense of community.

A strong sense of community is often attributed to the process of *bonding* in which a community focuses on all the attributes outlined above and develops a powerful sense of its own identity. This is often manifested in introversion, exclusivity, self-reinforcement and legitimation – the community becomes elite. The danger is that in doing so it loses the ability to engage with other communities. Effective communities thus combine the capacity to *bond* with the ability to *bridge*:

> Of all the dimensions along which forms of social capital vary, perhaps the most important is the distinction between *bridging* (or inclusive) and *bonding* (or exclusive). Some forms of social capital are, by choice or necessity, inward looking and tend to reinforce exclusive identities and homogeneous groups. Examples of bonding social capital include fraternal organizations, church-based women's reading groups, and fashionable country clubs. Other networks are outward looking and encompass people across diverse social cleavages. Examples of bridging social capital include the civil rights movement, many youth service groups, and ecumenical organizations. (Putnam, 2000, page 22)

> Bonding social capital constitutes a kind of sociological superglue, whereas bridging social capital provides a sociological WD-40. (Putnam, 2000, page 23)

A child or young person's life chances will be significantly determined by the extent to which they are involved in communities (school, neighbourhood and so on) which can both bond and bridge. The implication of the various possible relationships between bonding and bridging are shown in Figure 2.4.

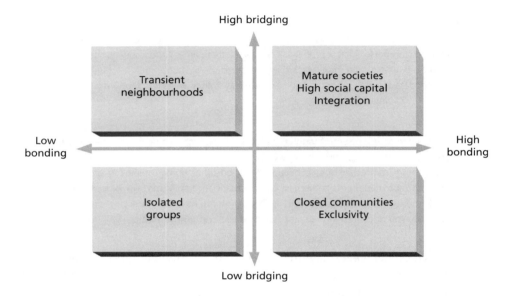

Figure 2.4 The implications of the permutations of bonding and bridging (after Halpern, 2005, page 21)

Combining high bonding and high bridging is essential if the life chances, educational achievement and academic attainment of children and young people are to be secured. Some possible implications of the relationship between social capital and educational success are found in the PISA report for 2000:

> ... student literacy levels are closely associated with socio-economic background, not just of the individual student but of his or her peers. Other things being equal, students do better if they go to school with people from more advantaged homes, and this is particularly true for individuals from lower socio-economic backgrounds.
>
> These results reinforce the importance of student background at the school level. They show that students attending schools where many other student are in the bottom quarter by socio-economic status are more likely than those at other schools to feel that they do not belong and to miss school or lessons. (page 14)

> The quarter of students from families with the lowest socio-economic status, students from lone parent families and foreign-born students are more likely to be disaffected.

> Students attending schools where there is a concentration of students from families with low socio-economic status are more likely to be disaffected, suggesting probable peer effects. (page 16)

Social capital is a direct determinant of educational success. More importantly, perhaps, it has a direct, real and concrete impact on life chances because, in most significant respects, it actually describes the lives we lead. Education both creates social capital and is a direct function of it:

> In sum, social capital appears to have a very large impact on educational attainment. A key mediating variable across levels is educational aspiration. Social networks and high expectations can stretch, encourage and inspire a child; though equally, the anti-educational norms of some communities and peer groups can do the reverse. On the face of it, the impact of social capital on educational attainment dwarfs that of the factors that governments and educational professionals normally argue about, such as financial resources, class sizes and teacher salaries. (Halpern, 2005, page 168)

Conclusion

This chapter has demonstrated what every parent, educator and probably most young people intuitively recognize – the school they attend and the teachers who teach them are far less significant than social class, poverty, the quality of family life and the level of social capital. Schools and teachers can and do make a difference – but, usually only when they do not work in conventional ways.

Schools and teachers work best when the social factors are most propitious. In fact, it could be argued that schools were only ever designed to work with the socially advantaged. The educational success of a school (by current measures) is directly correlated with the social success of the community it serves. As Adonis and Pollard (1997) argue:

> When Her Majesty's Chief Inspector of Schools identifies more than a quarter of those secondary schools classified as 'outstanding' as grammar schools (which account for only 0.7 per cent of the total), can society really continue to accept an education policy which refuses to acknowledge that state education is, by design, failing to offer anything approaching equal opportunities to children? (pages 62–63)

If equity and equal opportunities are to be real issues in the debate about the future of education, then the situation shown in Figure 2.5a will have to be changed to resemble that in Figure 2.5b.

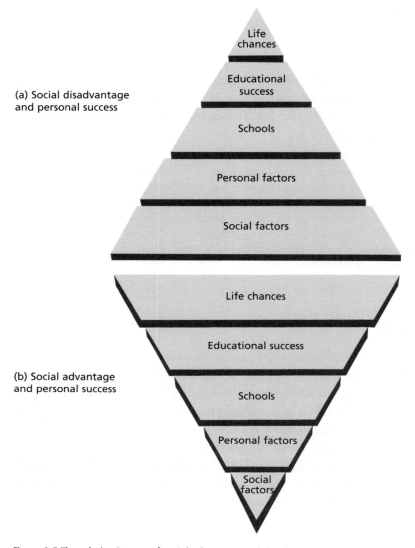

(a) Social disadvantage and personal success

(b) Social advantage and personal success

Figure 2.5 The relative impact of social advantage and disadvantage

The model shown in Figure 2.5 has (at least) two fundamental implications:

1. If schools are serious about 'educating the whole child', 'realizing potential' and 'maximizing achievement', then they will need to engage with the whole child or young person and his or her family and community.

2. It becomes even more important to ensure that the 20 per cent that schools can control is as effective and efficient as possible.

The first implication is the *raison d'être* of this book. Parts 2 and 3 are devoted to strategies to help schools engage with their communities to tackle the issues outlined in this chapter.

The second implication is already well understood and there are numerous sources available to provide advice on optimizing a school's effectiveness. However, it may be worth restating these principles in the context of this book. Schools that work in challenging circumstances need to have high confidence that they are safe. Not in the sense of security but rather in terms of confidence that the fundamentals are in place. Irrespective of the prevailing social factors, there is a range of factors that schools can and must accept direct responsibility for.

In this context it might be helpful to think of the school as a bridge linking the social and personal factors. Although any metaphor can be taken too far and over-elaborated, it does seem reasonable to argue that, like any bridge, a school needs to ensure that its design is appropriate to its context (unlike the Tacoma Narrows Bridge, which collapsed through wind-induced vibrations in 1940). It is also vital that the school is firmly embedded in each 'bank' and that all the different components are mutually supportive and interdependent.

Figure 2.6 offers an image of the school as a bridge with two main elements: effective leadership and efficient management; both designed to support high-quality learning and teaching.

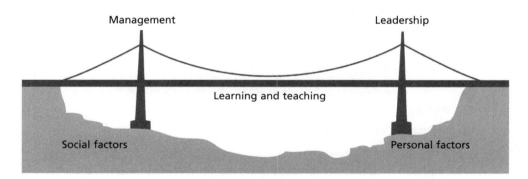

Figure 2.6 The school as a bridge

Each element needs to include the following components to be confident that the school is safe:

- Leadership:
  - the clear articulation of a common and shared purpose;
  - the articulation of values that are known, shared, understood and acted on by all members of the school community;

- a culture of high expectations and aspirations for all aspects of the school's life;
- high visibility and availability constantly reinforcing purpose and values;
- challenge and intervention to ensure effective learning and teaching;
- using every opportunity to support staff learning and development – celebrating success and focusing on improvement;
- communication and participation, student voice;
- modelling commitment, enthusiasm and energy.

- Management:
  - clear and explicit policies that are constantly referred to and used as the basis for monitoring and review;
  - efficient management of resources to ensure equity and availability;
  - focus on attendance, punctuality and readiness for work;
  - rich data available to inform learning and teaching and pastoral support;
  - inviting, well-presented and safe social and learning environments;
  - efficient organization of time and space to support learning and teaching.

- Teaching and learning:
  - clear protocols informing behaviour and engagement with learning;
  - shared understanding and appropriate deployment of models of effective learning and teaching;
  - challenging work supported by appropriate skills, strategies and resources;
  - explicit and agreed outcomes, clear success criteria;
  - rigorous, formative, developmental and consistent feedback and assessment;
  - targeted support, academic coaching;
  - a culture of learning, achievement and success.

All the topics listed above are directly under the control of the school. If they are in place then confidence in the school will increase and there is a greater possibility that the school will be able to engage with the social and personal factors.

3 The moral purpose of education

Introduction

The previous chapter explored the factors that inhibit or limit the life chances and educational success of children and young people. The approach was essentially practical – it explored the relationship between social factors and the possibility of personal success. Underpinning the chapter was an implicit assumption that every child and young person has a right to educational and personal success. This chapter explores that assumption and seeks to develop a moral case for equity in education.

There is, of course, a case for arguing that the pursuit of equity in any dimension of human life is both an illusion and a delusion. Virtually every human society is hierarchical and it would be wrong, if not actually cruel, to raise false aspirations. The advocates of the distribution curve can point to a mathematically precise balance in almost every natural and social dimension. The existence of an upper class implies middle and lower classes: wealth implies that there is also poverty. Quite apart from the issues of defining what is measured and how it is measured, such approaches imply a social determinism that seems to deny the possibility of moral choice. There are societies that have virtually eliminated child poverty; there are education systems that appear to have achieved equity and excellence. (Interestingly they are often in the same countries.)

Education is a social activity defined by personal and social choices – it is therefore a moral activity. One of the problems of British education is that it is deeply rooted in a moral framework that is the antithesis to any notion of equity or democracy. The malevolent influence of Plato continues to dominate much of educational thinking however subliminal or massaged it may be. The idea of the gold standard, the justification of a stratified society and the control and censorship of education can all be directly attributed to Plato. Those who argue for the incompatibility of excellence and equity are essentially perpetuating Plato's elitist and anti-democratic ideology. This chapter seeks to make the case for equity and social justice in education to underpin the case presented in Chapters 1 and 2. This chapter will therefore explore the following themes:

- Comparing and contrasting education and schooling
- The purpose of education
- Childhood
- Children's rights
- *Every Child Matters.*

Comparing and contrasting education and schooling

'When I use a word,' Humpty Dumpty said in a rather scornful tone, 'it means just what I choose it to mean – neither more nor less.' (Carroll, 1872, page 59)

One of the key problems in approaching this topic is that education and schooling are frequently used interchangeably, if not as actual synonyms. However, it quickly becomes apparent that the Department for Education is in fact concerned with institutions, content and outcomes, and that the mantra 'education, education, education' in fact means 'schools, schools, schools'. For the purposes of this discussion, schooling is defined as the formalized, commodified and bureaucratized component of education; in essence:

Schooling is a necessary but not sufficient component of education.

During the period of compulsory schooling, children and young people spend about 15 per cent of their life in schools. That time is powerful, fundamental and vital – yet, as Chapters 1 and 2 have demonstrated, it does not work equally well for all children. By the same corollary, access to education is also conditional on a wide range of factors. There are numerous formulations as to the nature of education and it is not the purpose of this chapter to add to the sum of human misery by proposing another formulation. For the purposes of this debate, however, it is proposed that an educated person is:

- literate, numerate and comfortable with information technology;
- capable of gathering, organizing and deploying information;
- able to analyse, synthesize and construct an argument to demonstrate understanding;
- able to think creatively and be comfortable with change, innovation and problem solving;
- confident about his or her own identity and value as a person and able to respect this in others;
- secure in personal relationships, able to work in groups and can contribute to the wider community;
- able to articulate personal values and spiritual understanding;
- able to demonstrate a deep respect for humanity and what it means to be human.

There is no doubt that schools have a significant role to play in the achievement of these aspirations. However, as was demonstrated in Chapter 2, schools have a limited and often deeply constrained capacity to respond to this agenda. Quite apart from the potentially inhibiting impact of social factors, schooling, of itself, may actually inhibit educating. This argument hinges on definitions and Table 3.1 offers a model to illustrate the differences between schooling and educating:

Table 3.1 Contrasting schooling and educating

Schooling	Educating
Linear	Adaptive
Fragmented	Holistic
Curriculum	Learning
Information	Knowledge
Quantitative	Qualitative
Bonding	Bridging
Outcomes	Processes
Control	Autonomy

In this model, schooling is perceived as an essentially linear process, the school day, week, term and year form a sequence of events. Progression is always age related by cohort and the sequence is automatic. Education, by contrast, is adaptive, contingent on time and place, often unpredictable and the result of complex interactions. Schooling tends to be fragmented by year and subject; education is a holistic experience, integrating all the different facets of developing understanding – moral, social and intellectual. In the same way, schooling has become synonymous with the delivery of a curriculum that is content and information centred. Education relates to the creation of knowledge – personal understanding and meaning. The measurement of the curriculum experience is invariably quantitative – outcomes, marks, grades and league tables. Education, by contrast, is concerned with more elusive, qualitative processes. As was discussed in Chapter 2, schools are dominated by bonding – by the need for institutional integrity. Education can occur only by bridging – building networks and relationships. A classic example of schooling as bonding is the secondary school curriculum which often fails to acknowledge the primary school experience and is then taught in subject silos to the extent that students are unable to make appropriate links between topics and themes.

In the final analysis, schooling is about control – of time, content, activity and outcome. Education is about the growth of personal autonomy, authenticity and the ability to accept responsibility for one's own learning and development.

Figure 3.1 simplifies and artificially polarizes the relationship between schooling and educating, but if the educational outcomes described above are to be achieved then the community has to be perceived as the dominant partner in the learning process.

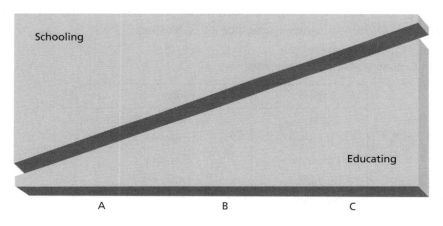

Figure 3.1 The balance between schooling and educating

At present, many secondary schools are probably at point A, most primary schools are at point B and many special schools are at point C. Chapter 7 explores the implications of this model in greater detail.

The tension between schooling and educating is a real one – most education professionals have felt frustrated by the compromises involved in schooling and have recognized that educating a young person is a complex, ambiguous process involving multiple perspectives. For Gardner (2006):

> We should remember that one of the most magnificent of human inventions is the invention of education – no other species educates its young as do we. At this time of

great change, we must remember the ancient value of education and preserve it – not just facts, data, information, but Knowledge, Understanding, Judgment, Wisdom. We must use the ancient arts and crafts of education to prepare youngsters for a world that natural evolution could not anticipate and which even we ourselves as conscious beings cannot fully envision either … And, as science and technology gain increasing hegemony over our lives and our minds, we must keep alive the important values of responsibility and humanity. (pages 234–235)

The purpose of education

It might seem more appropriate to title this section the purposes of education as, even within the definitions offered above, there is room for substantial debate about why we educate and what education is for. In many ways, the history of educational thinking can be broadly divided into those stressing the needs of society (for example Plato) and those who focus on the development of the individual (for example Rousseau). The dominance of schooling described in the previous section is largely a product of the triumph of the Platonists. However, there is a permanent tension between a number of imperatives in determining the focus, and so the nature, of an education system. The factors creating this tension might be (over-)simplified into three broad conceptual frameworks:

1. The purpose of education is to secure social justice through a focus on the rights and needs of the individual and so designing a system that responds to each person irrespective of social or economic status.

2. The purpose of education is to maximize the economic well-being of society by maximizing the number of highly qualified individuals who are ready for employment.

3. The purpose of education is to ensure the transmission of cultural norms and values from one generation to another through a focus on the historical and moral inheritance.

Of course, all systems will contain elements of all three components – what is significant is the relative proportion of each. Figure 3.2 shows an unlikely scenario of the three being in equilibrium.

In fact most education systems will have one or two of the components dominating the others, and it is the dominant purpose that will significantly and substantially determine the nature of schooling and so access to a wider definition of education. It is for the reader to explore the range of permutations of this model. In the context of this discussion, and in response to the issues raised in Chapter 2, it would seem that a commitment to social justice focused on meeting social and personal needs is the only possible response to the challenge of securing equity, inclusion and excellence.

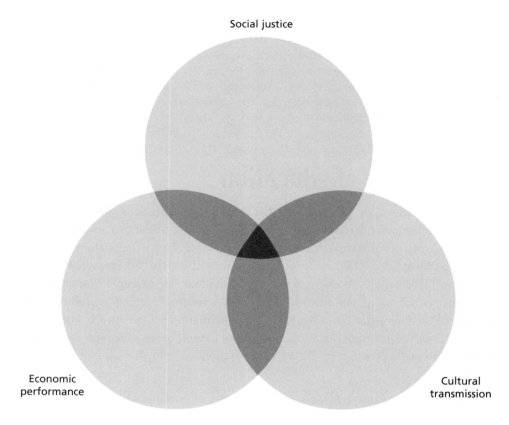

Figure 3.2 Reconciling the purposes of education

It may be significant that Finland, the best performing education system in Europe and one of the top three in the world, has a system based on social justice. Consider the following extract from *The Teacher's Professional Ethics*, published by the Trade Union of Education in Finland (2006, pages 3–4):

1. A humanistic conception of people and a respect for human beings form the underlying basis of ethical principles. The worth of a human being must be respected regardless, for example, of the person's gender, age, religion, origins, opinions or skills.

2. In relations between the teacher and group or the individual learner, as well as in the activities of the rest of the work community, justice must prevail. Justice encompasses equality, the avoidance of discrimination … The issue of justice always represents an element of the overall evaluation the teacher makes.

3. The point of departure for all social relations, however, is respect for the freedom that is intrinsic to a human being's worth.

4. The teacher accepts the learner, and strives to consider him or her as a unique individual.

There are many factors that can be offered to explain Finland's success. It is a relatively small, economically successful country with about 3.5 per cent child poverty, high social homogeneity, virtually no private education, no league tables, and a highly qualified and respected teaching profession that works to the principles outlined above. It might be argued that Finland achieves high performance because it focuses on social justice – not because it focuses on performance per se. In many respects Finland, and to some extent the other Scandinavian countries, has achieved success in schooling by focusing on the social and personal (the 80 per cent) rather than schooling (the 20 per cent). Systems that focus on the performance of schools do not appear to perform as well.

Education systems will always be microcosms of the society they serve – the moral hegemony of society will always be a dominant determinant of the nature of education. A society committed to social justice will have an education system which reflects that principle. A society that is driven by market forces and is thereby comfortable with institutionalized inequality will have an education system that reflects and reinforces those principles.

What is significant is the extent to which individual schools and communities can develop their own purpose within a national context. This is a key theme for Parts 2 and 3.

Childhood

Modern industrial societies have an ambivalent attitude to childhood and children. As Rabbi Julia Neuberger (2005) observes:

> We have a strange attitude to children in Britain. Children were given legal protection relatively late in the UK, and we still prefer children to be seen and not heard. (page 124)

> At the same time, many of us are now loathe to have children at all and increasingly see children as a nuisance. Britain is not a family friendly country, and parents often see themselves as pariahs when out with their children. (page 125)

> We can tolerate a huge amount of generalized risk to children and young people, but throw up our hands in horror at the news of one child beaten to death by his or her parents – even though this is common place.
> We can tolerate widespread and general misery, despite knowing what it might lead to in terms of suicide and breakdown, but find it hard when one individual or agency is blamed. (page 191)

Although there are countless exceptions to the rule, it does seem to be better to be a child in Asian, African and Mediterranean cultures compared to many Western societies. One possible explanation is the tension in the view of childhood; being perceived as either valid of itself or as a preparation, a stage, on the route to adulthood:

> One fundamental line of division lies between thinking of childhood as a state and thinking of it as a stage. This is the distinction between viewing children as 'being' and as 'becoming'. On the former conception childhood is a free-standing, independently defined condition; it is not adulthood but its character is not exhausted by this privative fact. On the latter conception childhood occupies a place, or level, within a broader narrative and derives its significance from that narrative – more especially from what succeeds or supplants childhood in the longer story; childhood is not yet adulthood and derives much, if not all, of its character from this fact. (Archard , 2005, page 92)

If childhood is a stage, then it is much more likely that an economic/performance model of education will dominate. If childhood is perceived as a state, then the issue of rights becomes far more significant. There is a school of thought which argues that a key role of education is to lift children out of poverty and improve their life chances – through the old assisted places scheme, or having access to grammar schools or by attending an academy. While laudable, this approach could be seen to deny the value and integrity of childhood itself – education as a means of improvement for the few rather than the entitlement of the many.

This focus on deferred gratification has worrying theological undertones and serves to diminish the integrity of a child's actual experience and diminish his or her personhood. To define childhood as 'not-adulthood' or to see the child as an 'adult-in-waiting' is as inappropriate as a sentimental or romantic view of childhood as innocence. Children are vulnerable, they do lack knowledge, skills, aptitudes and abilities, and at the same time they are growing and developing (or should be) physically, socially, emotionally and intellectually. This growth is a complex interaction of the personal and the social – the neurological at one extreme and becoming part of a community at the other.

Those who see childhood as a stage would presumably not argue for stages in terms of rights: as a child moves closer to young adulthood so they become more entitled to equity. While full participation in a democracy, in other words becoming a citizen, is available at 18, it does not follow that there is an incremental entitlement to the benefits of living in a democratic society. (It is worth remembering that not so many years ago the age of consent was 21. What happened, apart from legislation, to change 18 year olds from children to adults?)

It may be that stage and state is an artificial dichotomy. Human beings are going through stages throughout their lives and they do so at different rates. Equally, there are many adults who are vulnerable in different ways – does anybody who reads this not have a special need of some sort? Puberty used to be seen as a defining transitional phase in human development, and in many societies marked 'the entry to adulthood' – changes in the biological stage have not, properly, been reflected in changes in the social stage. So, inevitably, the argument becomes contingent on context, and what is very clear is that the nature of the community in which a child grows up has a profound impact on the perception of childhood. This is not to argue for cultural relativism but to reinforce the importance of community.

A powerful example of how a community can reconcile the developmental notion of stage with the rights of state is to be found in the Italian community of Reggio Emilia. Early years education in Reggio Emilia has the following characteristics, which make it one of the most respected and emulated approaches in the world:

- The town of Reggio Emilia has a long tradition of co-operative and inclusive strategies and social policies that actively support families and children.
- The Reggio approach does not see the child as a tabula rasa, rather as a person of unlimited potential eager to learn, to engage with the world and capable of taking responsibility for his or her own learning.
- Children are seen as 'active participants' in the development of their identities and abilities through their relationships and interactions.
- The early years approach of Reggio is not about preparation for school but is seen as a distinct developmental phase.
- Teachers are trained to facilitate and enable children to build on their own interests. The concept of *Progettazione* (as defined in the following point) is about emergent learning, driven by children and so developing cognitive growth – 'a spiral of knowledge'.
- Learning is not constrained by time, subjects or the teacher's agenda.
- The Reggio approach is a 'pedagogy of relationships' centred on participants and interaction. Families do not get involved with the school; they are partners in the educational process.

The Reggio approach is a practical example of education rather than schooling, of a shared sense of purpose focused on the individual and a deep respect for the child as a person learning with and through a dynamic community.

Children's rights

The success of early years education in Reggio Emilia can be largely attributed to a combination of collective community action and political will. Most importantly, there was a coherent and systematic philosophy of childhood, education and learning that was translated into practical action. It may also be significant that Reggio Emilia is a distinct geographical community, relatively prosperous, with a rich cultural heritage, a strong sense of community identity and a history of voting for socialist political parties, in other words, many of the ingredients of high social capital.

Where such propitious circumstances are missing, then a more formal, legalistic and explicit approach may be necessary.

An important starting point for any discussion of children's rights is the United Nations' Convention on the Rights of the Child (CRC): as Archard (2004) notes:

> The CRC gives children rights to, interalia, freedom of expression, association, thought, conscience and religion, protection against abuse and violence, enjoyment of the highest attainable standard of health, education, rest and leisure, protection from economic exploitation and hazardous work.
>
> The CRC is important in the following respect. It represents children as the subjects of rights. Children are recognised in a major international covenant as moral and legal subjects possessed of fundamental entitlements. They are acknowledged as having agency and as having a voice that must be listened to. (page 58)

However, as Archard goes on to point out, there remains systematic, worldwide abuse of children which takes many different forms: from slavery through forced prostitution, to serving as child soldiers. Many of the states that have signed the convention have not integrated it into domestic legislation. Also, there is no means of enforcing the provisions of the CRC.

Two articles of the CRC are particularly relevant to the present discussion:

Article 29

1. States Parties agree that the education of the child shall be directed to:

   a. The development of the child's personality, talents and mental and physical abilities to their fullest potential;

   b. The development of respect for human rights and fundamental freedoms, and for the principles enshrined in the Charter of the United Nations;

   c. The development of respect for the child's parents, his or her own cultural identity, language and values, for the national values of the country in which the child is living, the country from which he or she may originate, and for civilizations different from his or her own;

   d. The development of respect for the natural environment.

Article 30

In those States in which ethnic, religious or linguistic minorities or persons of indigenous origin exist, a child belonging to such a minority or who is indigenous shall not be denied the right, in community with other members of his or her group, to enjoy his or her own culture, to profess and practise his or her own religion, or to use his or her own language.

The tension between the care and protection of children, in other words the principles related to stage, are increasingly seen as being insufficient; the Sixth Kilbrandon Child Care Lecture (2004) argues for the importance of reconciling the rights of stage with the entitlement of state:

> Attitudes towards children have undergone some dramatic positive changes since the beginning of the last century in Europe and the international community has, to a large extent, acknowledged and recognised that children need special care and protection because they are vulnerable. Yet, at the same time we are witnessing increasing awareness that children are not only in need of care and special protection but that they are also legal subjects and holders of rights. Making them aware of their position in society and of the rights and obligations they hold is a necessary corollary to this development.

In other words it is not enough to simply prevent inappropriate things happening to children – there has to be positive intervention to secure fundamental entitlement. Two significant and closely related initiatives in England recognize this need to move from the passive reliance on rights to the active engagement with entitlement.

The first of these is the appointment of a children's commissioner – a post copied from Scandinavian practice and installed in Wales, Scotland and Northern Ireland. The mission and vision of the Office of the Children's Commissioner for England (2006) is:

> Our mission is:
>
> To be the voice for all children and young people in England. We will use our independence and dedication to look after the interests of children and young people. We will do this by making sure that everyone involves children and young people in matters that affect them. We will protect and improve their lives by working with and influencing society, parents and carers, the media, politicians and those who work with children and young people. We will promote debate on changing the world children live in.
>
> Vision:
>
> Our vision is for a society where all children and young people:
>
> – are encouraged, nurtured and safeguarded
>
> – have their views actively sought, listened to and acted upon

– have their rights upheld

– are truly at the centre of policy and practice. (page 11)

Central to the work of the Children's Commissioner is the *Every Child Matters* agenda. This is explored in detail in the next section.

Every Child Matters

It would be wrong to underestimate the importance, in England, of the Children Act (2004) and the implementation of the *Every Child Matters'* strategy.

The Children Act represents a potential watershed in social attitudes towards children and young people. In essence, it has the capacity to move from an approach based on 'find and fix' to one based on 'predict and prevent'. It is very difficult to establish the provenance of this precept but it coincides with many of the precepts of quality management and the common-sense dictum 'prevention is better than cure'. The prevailing management philosophy in most public services in England over recent years has been predominantly 'find and fix', in other words react to a problem. The Children Act and, in particular, *Every Child Matters* introduces a philosophy of 'predict and prevent'. Chapter 2 demonstrated that educational failure and diminished life chances can be very largely predicted. The combination of low social class, poverty, dysfunctional family life and living in a community with low social capital has a direct correlation with poor educational achievement. There is a direct causal relationship and therefore prediction is possible. If failure can be predicted with confidence then it becomes possible to introduce preventive strategies. This is already being demonstrated in the major restructuring of children's services at local level in England that has been taking place since 2004.

More important than the restructuring is the fundamental change in language that *Every Child Matters* has enabled and, crucially, the development of a shared conceptual framework. It could be argued that, for the first time in England, there is an explicit moral code that has the potential to inform policy and practice. One of the factors that gives *Every Child Matters* real credibility is that it was based on a large-scale consultation process:

When we consulted children, young people and families, they wanted the Government to set out a positive vision of the outcomes we want to achieve. The five outcomes which mattered most to children and young people were:

- *being healthy*: enjoying good physical and mental health and living a healthy lifestyle
- *staying safe*: being protected from harm and neglect

- *enjoying and achieving*: getting the most out of life and developing the skills for adulthood
- *making a positive contribution*: being involved with the community and society and not engaging in anti-social or offending behaviour
- *economic well-being*: not being prevented by economic disadvantage from achieving their full potential in life.

(HM Government, 2003, pages 6–7)

The five components of *Every Child Matters* provide a powerful synthesis of many of the principles outlined in the previous section of this chapter and a direct response to the issues identified in Chapters 1 and 2. What is clear is that no school can achieve the *Every Child Matters'* outcomes on its own. This implies a move from bonding to bridging through new approaches to engagement, collaboration and intervention. This, of itself, involves a fundamental rethinking of the nature of school leadership and governance. Some of the specific implications of *Every Child Matters* can be found in the following summary:

Being healthy
- understanding personal health and fitness;
- making healthy choices about diet and lifestyle;
- strategies to enhance mental and emotional health;
- awareness of issues relating to sexual health and drug abuse;
- developing a positive self-image.

Staying safe
- strategies for personal safety and security;
- freedom from bullying, intimidation and abuse;
- freedom from discrimination;
- access to appropriate support and intervention;
- living and learning through secure relationships.

Enjoying and achieving
- access to balanced and relevant learning experiences;
- support in learning how to learn;
- a culture of high aspirations and expectations;
- opportunities for success and achievement;
- an integrated and developmental curriculum;
- support for cognitive, social, cultural, emotional, moral and spiritual growth;
- personalized support.

Making a positive contribution

- participate in and contribute to all aspects of school life;
- share in social learning, activities and projects;
- volunteer and provide services to the wider community;
- develop tolerance and respect;
- engage in social, cultural and sporting activities.

Economic well-being

- opportunities to develop skills, abilities and interests;
- awareness of career and employment possibilities;
- awareness of economic and social options.

Many schools will be able to point to the fact that they meet these criteria, in school, for most children. What *Every Child Matters* does is to first raise the challenge of every child and young person and not just in school – rather in every aspect of their lives. That is the challenge that the rest of this book seeks to respond to.

Conclusion

This chapter has explored the moral case for education engaging with the community, in the same way that Chapters 1 and 2 presented a case on practical grounds. Although there are numerous formulations and levels of abstraction, the rest of this book draws on a number of fundamental propositions derived from this chapter:

1. Every child and young person is a unique individual with explicit rights and entitlements.
2. Those rights and entitlements should not be compromised by accidents of birth, economic or social circumstances.
3. It is the moral and professional duty of all those working with children and young people to maximize their life chances and personal achievement by working for social justice.

Part 2

Building social capital

4 Social capital and learning

Introduction

If you want to build a ship, don't drum up the people to gather wood, divide the work and give orders. Instead, teach them to yearn for the vast and endless sea. (Antoine de Saint Exupery, *The Wisdom of the Sands*)

There is much being said today about the importance of building learning communities in our schools:

A community of people is a place, rooted in the biosphere, rife with activity, mutual respect, and the recognition that everyone in that place is responsible for and accountable to one another, because the lives of all are interdependent.
A community that learns, in our view, shares a mutual commitment with its schools. The community is a nurturing, supportive, sometimes challenging, but always caring container wrapped around the school and the development of children. (Senge et al., 2000, page 461)

Yet, any understanding of semantics will caution us to be careful as to what we are talking about. A learning community is not always the same. You can build a learning community in many different ways to accomplish many different purposes. For our purposes we want to build a learning community that sees each person in the community as a resource for education, born a 'lean mean learning machine', willing and able to support the survival, development and transformation of each individual and the community as a whole.

This conception is significantly different from the learning communities that are promoted in many school settings today. Those learning communities are intended to make the school more effective as an institution. And families and communities are not institutions; they are more properly pictured as organisms.

This chapter will explore how the principles of building social capital can be applied to support learning. In this context learning is used in the widest possible sense but is seen primarily as a social process through which understanding is achieved. This chapter will focus on:

- Models of learning
- A model for learning in relationship
- School-based strategies to secure engagement in learning
- Building a learning community.

Models of learning

All learning is relational and therefore takes place within a group. Most current models of learning forget the fact that learning is primarily a social process. We learn in order to meet our goals. Educational goals can vary widely among communities yet in Western societies, such as England, Australia and the US, school has been increasingly focused on the goal of maximizing individual knowledge and skill as a resource for enhancing personal wealth and success. This emphasis has produced a model of learning that is supported by current testing regimes internationally: the push to make citizens more economically competitive globally by emphasizing maths and science training, and by the tendency to perceive education as a commodity.

A community, from family to neighbourhood, town, precinct or city, has a very limited and focused role to play when the bottom line is individual achievement and access to educational opportunity.

Education in contemporary society results in a model of learning that goes something like as follows. Every individual, regardless of circumstances (physical, mental, social, ethnic or economic) can apply themselves and educate themselves to achieve the highest status and wealth the society has to offer. This belief is justified by finding any one individual from the most 'challenging' circumstances who has successfully climbed the social and economic ladder as proof that any other individual could do the same and that such achievement is in fact the major goal of education in the community. This model can be represented with a simple triangle, where the tip or top of the triangle represents high social and economic success and standing, and the base of the triangle represents the vast majority of people in the community who have only moderate to nearly non-existent social standing or wealth. Many industrial societies find that most of the leaders and up to 20 per cent of the wealth in that nation reside in only 1 per cent to 3 per cent of the total population, whereas the vast majority find themselves sharing very little of the success or access to wealth and opportunity the

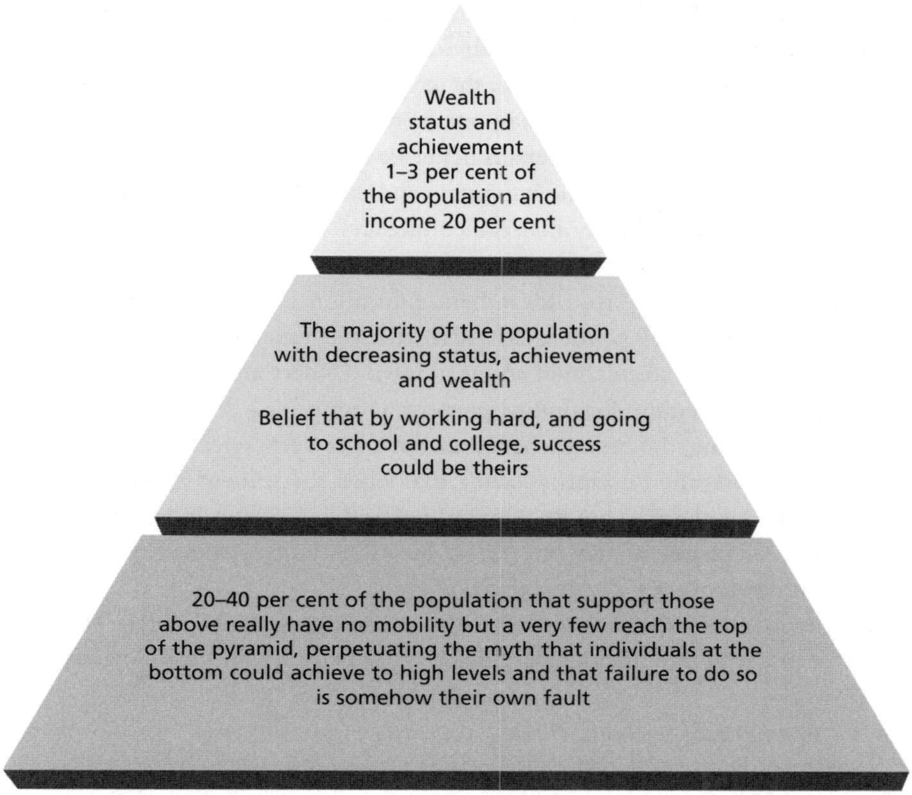

Figure 4.1 The dominant model of education in society

nation claims to have. This triangle can take a more flattened shape in nations such as Finland, Sweden and Norway, yet the basic model of learning remains the same. In the model shown in Figure 4.1, governments, towns and families structure schools to support individual acquisition of the knowledge and skill needed to move up the ladder. The result is that we have built 'learning communities' that see education as an individual resource in limited supply that, if acquired, developed or protected, can result in high social status, increasing and often unlimited wealth, and increased access to society's benefits. In this model, productive learning always results in social and economic gain.

The result of the current model of learning is competition among individuals, families and communities for the knowledge, skill and access to training that will provide a person with a marked advantage in economic spheres. Such a single-minded focus on attainment and acquisition makes education a game of winners and losers, and places the attention solely on the individual where family and community are simply resources that work for or against individual success.

A different model of learning would be characterized more by a circle than a triangle, more as a social process than individual acquisition, and more focused on the relationships in which we learn than on the content, knowledge or skill to be learned. In this model, found in every society in one form or another, educational attainment, wealth and status do not make a person better or more important than others. There are many ways to find and pursue happiness and contribute to self- and community learning and betterment. North American cultures refer to this view of society in terms of the medicine wheel. Life is composed of stages, each as important as the other and each feeding and receiving from the others. Education is necessary and available to everyone. The purpose of youth is to learn who you are, what is true and what is beautiful, how to serve, create, build and tear down. Understanding the cycles of life in fours provides a curriculum for finding purpose and meaning throughout one's life. In this model of learning, the best teacher is not found in a few selected universities only. This model supports the Buddhists' saying that when the student is ready the teacher will appear. The emphasis is not on competition and acquisition in isolation from the circumstances or stages of life one faces. Relations and relationships matter, and learning is understood as a dynamic social process.

Such a process is inextricably linked with the concept of social capital. The concept itself is still contentious and emergent; Field (2003) defines it in the following terms:

> The theory of social capital is, at heart, most straightforward. Its central thesis can be summed up in two words: relationships matter. By making connections with one another, and keeping them going over time, people are able to work together to achieve things that they either could not achieve by themselves, or could only achieve with great difficulty. People connect through a series of networks and they tend to share common values with other members of these networks ... (page 1)

Field's work also goes on to demonstrate the link between social capital and achievement:

> In general, the research suggests that the influence of social capital is a benign one, in that it is associated with higher levels of performance ... (page 49)

and

> ... we can conclude with some confidence that there is a close relationship between people's social networks and their educational performance. (page 50)

An alternative definition that for some schools is closer to their understanding of social capital, particularly where young people are concerned, is that of 'social energy' as 'social capital in action'. This is a notion developed by Albert Hirschmann (1984, pages 42–57) to describe grass roots movements, particularly in developing countries.

He described the elements of social energy as being:

- friendship
- ideals and values
- ideas and creativity.

In this model of learning, there is no one best pathway to happiness and success. Education is a community resource and everyone is a needed learner. Life is broken down into fours: four seasons, four stages of life, four directions, four elements and so on, representing the cyclical nature of learning and life. The circle contains the elements just described but it does not dominate educational provision as it does in most modern nation states today.

Figure 4.2 Learning as a relational process

It is an important and significant change in perspective to see learning primarily as a social process. This perspective is required when looking at education in the context of community. Productive learning is no longer measured solely in terms of competitive advantage, as indicated by test scores and degrees, but is more a mix of advancing individual knowledge and skill in service to both the individual and the collective, realizing the interdependence between individual satisfaction and achievement and community vitality. These perspectives are summarized by Rabbi Jonathan Sacks (2000):

> Community values the 'we' as well as the I, it restores the dignity of agency and responsibility, and above all it tells us where to begin if we seek a better world. For some time I have felt the ever urgent need for a national conversation to seek a more effective

interaction between our schools and families, governments and local communities –
between our institutions and our local sources of moral energy. (page 15)

Building learning communities that serve multiple educational goals requires a certain understanding of the relationship between learning and the community. Guiding learning in the community, when the goals of equity, wellness and achievement are of equal importance, requires that all stakeholders build relationships with each other that increase educational opportunity and success, first for children and youths and then for all members of the community.

Michael Fullan (1999) has explored school improvement strategies for most of his career. Recently, after years of enquiry and research he boldly stated, 'Any educational reform strategy that improves relationships has a chance of succeeding; any strategy that does not is doomed to fail':

On the community-building side, these schools and organizations know that the quality of relationships is central to success. Success is only possible if organizational members develop trust and compassion for each other, i.e. for others different than themselves (given that diversity is built in). If you understand the deep meaning of achieving diversity *and* community building, you avoid fatal mistakes. (Fullan, 1999, page 37)

As we have just suggested, relationships that make a difference in learning are inspired by a particular kind of relationship. Relationships that make a difference in learning produce partnerships that make learning respectfully together a reality. These partnered relationships result in mutual ownership of our experience and learning: individually and collectively.

Research in business, education, human relations, psychology and organizational development demonstrates the transformative power of positive relationships on our lives and communities. Social capital is a recent construct intended to help us describe, develop and protect these positive relationships. In examining numerous social and educational programmes from the perspective of how to 'spread what works', Lisbeth Schorr (1997) in her ground-breaking work, *Common Purpose*, concludes that it was replicating relationship building that accounted for success, not just the transfer of an idea or product. Robert Putnam, in his examination of 13 communities that have found ways to 'work better together', states that developing relationships is the central and transformative challenge in building learning communities that can address the issues facing our schools and communities in today's world (Putnam, 2003).

As Fullan (2001) muses, 'Effective leaders work on their own and others' emotional development. There is no greater skill for sustainable improvement' (page 74). Each of us can recount from personal experience the factors that turn us away from developing equitable, respectful and democratic relationships in our schools and communities. It is the purpose of this book to help us, individually and collectively, to direct our energy and skill towards the creation of trusting relationships among and between all members of the community and school. Without these relationships there is little hope of creating the learning communities we desire.

A model for learning in relationship

Since all learning is relational it is important to understand the relational qualities that nurture the learning that supports the outcomes that schools and communities collectively seek.

Once again, education will only improve when we focus on building better teaching and learning relationships within the school and across the community. We cannot continue to make a commitment to educating the whole person while ignoring the relationships in which all learning occurs. While attempts are being made to address the social, physical and spiritual needs, as well as the academic requirements of learners, these efforts often result in more isolation. What is called for is a strategy to help us meet the articulated visions we have created to educate the whole person.

How do we improve our focus on relationships in educational settings? What is the strategy to make relationships the context for teaching and learning? We must move beyond the simplistic evaluation of relationships as being good or bad. The RelationaLearning™ model outlined below suggests that all learning progresses through four levels of relationship. We are always in a relationship but the quality of that relationship and therefore the quality of learning varies greatly. As we move through each level, we can identify the added power that relationships can bring to our learning. Figure 4.3 describes these four levels.

Phase I: Recognition

At the recognition level (the level at which most teaching currently occurs) content is explained through lecture or attained by reading or

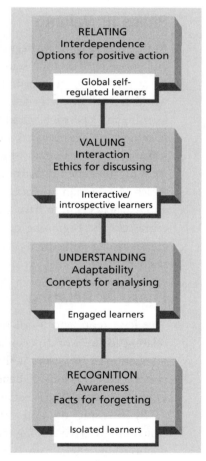

Figure 4.3 Synopsis of the four phases of RelationaLearning™

downloading information from a computer. At this level, the memorization of facts can and often does occur. This information is of little value, however, unless learning is advanced to another level by applying the learning to a project or problem, and refining it through interaction and interrelationship. If not taken to higher relational levels, the learner has simply obtained facts for forgetting.

Phase II: Understanding

At the understanding level, the facts or concepts are tested through application, interaction and interrelationship. Facts are not simply for short-term memorization. They can now be understood as they relate to other facts and concepts as well as other human beings and the world at large. They are now making sense because they seem to be relevant, useful and of potential value to our lives.

Phase III: Valuing

At the valuing level, we begin to incorporate the concepts acquired at recognition level and appreciated at understanding level with our personal, internal value structures. We are again testing; this time testing the fit of the new learning to the way we deal with our world and our everyday choices. We have now begun to discern the overall value of the learning to us personally and have begun to translate that learning outwards. This level is significant because it is here that we begin to experience the connection of the learning to other human beings as well. We know that we do not live in isolation and we must integrate this learning with our lives and the lives of others. This is the level at which true human potential for RelationaLearning™ begins to emerge. Both students and teachers begin to have a different experience. Both parties are learning. This level represents the beginning of self-governance by the learner. This is the beginning of creativity and authenticity. This is the level at which the learner begins to decide what really matters.

Phase IV: Relating

This level represents a call to the self, to find one's own place, way and meaning in relating to the world personally and collectively. At this level, the learner views any interaction in new ways with new options. At the relating level, options are apparent and the learner is making beneficial choices for him- or herself and others. At this level, everyone's experience is equally shared with others in meaningful, productive ways.

By focusing on and improving relationships, schools can begin making a contribution to developing the entire community's capacity to learn. Schools can make relationships their core business. A way to begin is to look at the curriculum relationally. Based on the model just described, the development of equitable, interdependent relationships can be achieved when schools make at least four relationships the centre of their work. These are:

1. the student's relationship to the subject;
2. the student's relationship to other students;
3. the student's relationship to the teacher; and
4. the student's relationship to the wider community.

Using these four relationships as curriculum brings the entire staff together in an effort to enlarge and enrich the social capital within the school itself. As staff members examine their practice, they determine which critical relationship or relationships are being served by a programme, activity or lesson. By modelling relational learning at the school level, the school shows by action how learning can be enhanced beyond the school.

At Wodonga South Primary School, in regional Victoria, Australia, the staff explored in depth the RelationaLearning™ model and has now organized the entire school from vision to practice around teaching and learning relationships.

Their model is simple and easy to understand and sets the stage for working more closely with the parents and the community.

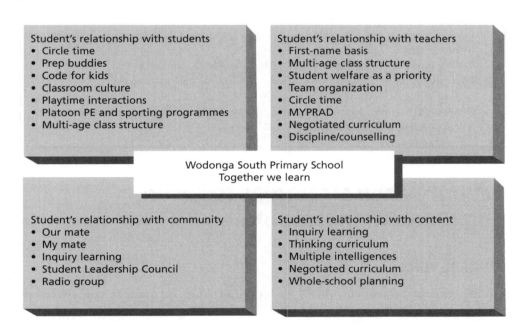

Figure 4.4 Together we learn

Note: MYPRAD = Middle years research and development

> **Wodonga South Primary School**
> **RELATIONAL LEARNING**
>
> This document outlines the thinking and action that underpins our operation in terms of promoting relationships at Wodonga Primary School.
>
> *Beliefs and understandings*
> We believe relationships underpin the success of effective school operation.
> We believe positive relationships are essential to achieve a quality learning environment.
> We understand relationships operate on mutual respect.
> We understand quality teaching relationships come from knowing our students.
> We understand that developing relationships fosters a culture of lifelong learning.
> We understand that students become engaged learners when they form a relationship with the content.
> We believe in building relationships with the community.
>
> *Therefore we will*
> Promote positive relationships as part of our school's culture and identity.
> Actively pursue and promote positive relations at every opportunity, with all members of the school community.
> Act as role models in our relationships with others.
> Work to foster personal relationships with each of our students.
> Develop pedagogy and programmes that enhance and maximize relationships with and between students.
> Develop curriculum that meets student interest and relates to them personally.
> Develop ongoing and incidental links with the community at every opportunity.
>
> This document profiles the programmes and opportunities for promoting relationships at our school [as shown in Figure 4.4].

School-based strategies to secure engagement in learning

Student voice

Schools engage in student voice, student leadership or student empowerment programmes for a range of reasons:

- These programmes lie at the heart of building community and social capital within the school.

- These programmes build hope – and the belief that students can make a difference.

- These programmes build trust within the school community.

- Students are a powerful resource in the development of school and community partnerships.
- Investing in student leadership potential is a direct long-term investment in the community.
- These programmes are a direct investment in growing leadership potential.
- These programmes build internal and external social capital.

Students who are engaged in student voice work are involved in a range of ways. They may be on a student council or student appointment board. Some schools involve students on change teams and improvement boards. Students support teaching and learning through mentoring new teachers and supporting younger learners. In some schools, students are seen as catalysts to develop bridging social capital through being school–community ambassadors.

Student involvement helps to build a shared set of norms and values within the school community and to generate the sense of hope that 'students matter'. They can also help to stimulate social capital outside the school in a range of ways. Local authorities can employ staff to work with young people and consult on issues around education, leisure, recreation, transport, housing and health. Arts and cultural programmes can support children and young people to make multimedia products, stage performances and events that allow them to express their points of view to the wider public. Community organizations can engage young people in identifying local issues of concern to them, designing solutions and implementing their recommendations.

Kaye Johnson worked as a research associate at NCSL in 2004 and took 'children's voices' as her theme. She sees that making a public and strong statement about student voice within and beyond the school is an essential first step and needs to be seen as a broader move towards democratization of the school with its community. (NCSL, 2004a, page 2)

Student leadership has been a central core purpose of a number of school networked learning communities, and a student leadership programme co-created and developed by students is thriving in London. All these initiatives conclude that the intellectual and social capital of students is being wasted in schools, and that enabling student voice and empowerment is a powerful means of building social capital both within and outside the school.

Extended learning

The development of extended services and, in particular, the opportunity to extend learning beyond the school day, week and year provides us with a real opportunity to engage in the development of social capital.

Extended learning, in particular, exists at the margins of formal schooling and as such enables 'softer' entry points than the mainstream organization. To use Robert Putnam's (2000) terminology, extended learning and extra-curricular activities provide 'on-ramps' to enable the school and community to engage together and build up the levels of trust, friendship, ownership and commitment that feed the growth of social capital. When schools and communities work together:

- they build ownership – students, teachers, families and communities can work together to develop ideas and make them happen;
- they foster social entrepreneurship – a club can develop into a local business or, through a 'time bank' scheme, a range of talents in the community can be drawn on;
- they foster a collective engagement in learning;
- they promote and practise shared accountability and responsibility; young people in particular move from being the consumers of a service to active contributors in its development;
- they grow at the margins of formal schooling and as such can be collectively owned;
- they connect young people within the community and are not exclusively open to those students who attend a specific school;
- they encourage active civic engagement with the community through volunteering and active citizenship;
- they build the confidence in the capacity of the community to engage in the learning and well-being of young people;
- they are fun.

In the US, the work of Robert Putnam has provided informal educators, alongside a discussion of social capital, with a powerful rationale for their activities. These informal educators feel that, at last, learning beyond the classroom is now given the same recognition as that within the classroom, and the value of voluntarily joining and being involved in organized, informal groups is seen as having a significant impact on individual health and well-being. It has also been observed that the quality of day-to-day interactions in the classroom is enhanced through a greater emphasis on the development of extra-curricular activities involving teams and groups.

Parental engagement

The building of social capital in schools can also have a profound effect on building engagement with parents; parents have a positively disproportionate effect on children's attainment, particularly in the early years of schooling. Social capital helps to develop shared norms and values between the school and the home, thus reducing the disconnection between these two domains in a child's life.

The San Francisco Unified School District has recognized the importance of closing this gap and has made active efforts to generate parental participation in learning and school, culminating in a city-wide parental empowerment conference that has attracted over 800 parents in each of the five years it has been held. As a result of this social capital work on building shared norms and values, parents in the city are seen not as dysfunctional, uncaring or unsupportive but as partners who make a meaningful contribution to their children's lives and the life of the community and school.

Friendships

Children's friendships within and outside school are also an important source of social capital and one which schools could do more to nurture.

The Economic and Social Research Council's Families and Social Capital Research Group has published a study into the way that children's social networks are sustained through schooling and what they contribute to local 'social capital', or the number of friends people have.

The report finds that just over one-third of secondary school students identify a close friend as one with whom they had gone to primary school. For most of the rest, although the primary school friendships had tailed off, they had used these early friendships as social capital to help them in the transition to secondary school.

In addition, older siblings and cousins make up social capital for children to draw on when moving from primary to secondary school, often providing support if the child is bullied. On the other hand, children can help to develop their parents' social networks because parents meet each other through their children (Weller, 2005).

At the heart of social capital and at the heart of learning is trust.

Schools as public spaces

Schools cannot be agencies of social capital unless they are public spaces. They cannot promote social capital unless they encourage connection, engagement and interaction within and beyond the school. How schools operate in order that they are perceived as spaces that the public 'co-own' is a challenge. According to Craig and O'Leary (2005) public spaces have characteristics as shown in Table 4.1.

Table 4.1 Characteristics of public spaces

Open	Closed
At times surprising	Characterized by routine and little 'surprise'
Inviting	Intimidating
Can be co-opted in the public interest	Not responsive to public interest
Are brought to life by the people who use them	Are brought to life by the people who work in them

Perhaps an unfair criticism but one that needs to be addressed if schools are going to be seen as agents of social capital development. One solution may be for schools to foster the growth of third spaces, in which they can meet with communities on an equal basis and on neutral territory. It might also mean looking at ways in which 'ordinary life' can be allowed back into school on equal terms. This may sometimes require giving up space when it's at a premium. Margaret Carter, deputy head at Thomas Hepburn School, Gateshead, is clear on the value of building social capital and what takes priority:

> If you've allocated a space to the community, it's important they have that space. If there's a group that have a room every Tuesday and the school needs it one week, I can't just say 'you can't have it this week, the school needs it'. If you're giving a commitment to the community, that commitment has to be just as strong as if it were to the school, otherwise they'll feel like you're just putting up with them. If you felt like that you wouldn't go into someone's house would you? (NCSL, 2006b, page 14)

Other schools report opening the doors and then being amazed at the floodgates that open in response to this:

> Our parents now know that the door is open always. And it can be difficult sometimes but to encourage that you do have to go with the flow. It has changed completely. Three years ago seven or eight people came, last year we had fifty. This year we were in the middle of a torrential downpour and we put fifty chairs out just in case. We stopped counting after two hundred and fifty came in.' (Therese Allen, headteacher, Wychwood School, in NCSL, 2006b, page14)

Building a learning community

Building a community is the first step in establishing a learning community. Families and communities are the ground-level generators and preservers of values and ethical systems. Educational provision is built on these values and ethical systems. No society can remain vital or even survive without a reasonable base of shared values – and such values are not established by edict from lofty levels of the society, although governments often try. They are generated chiefly in the family, school, church and other intimate settings in which people deal with one another face to face.

Therefore, community building activities should focus on developing:

- the importance of the sense and experience of community;
- the extraordinary need that individuals have for identification with and empowerment within their own surroundings;
- the experience of belonging and personal agency;

- the opportunity for heartfelt face-to-face conversation;
- the collective exploration and application of values;
- the negotiation of common purpose;
- the exercise of shared leadership and group accountability;
- the opportunity for developing relationships that cross social, organizational and role barriers, and that spark collaboration.

Sparking collaboration

School and community leaders know that problem solving requires collaboration across departments and divisions – and not just because innovations often come from these joint projects. Changing an organization's or group's dynamics requires collective commitments to new courses of action, lest local decisions, taken in isolation, undermine that change. New strategies are possible when various types of conversations are held about combining assets in different ways.

Thus, Greg Dyke's (former director general of the BBC) first major initiative, announced within two months of his arrival, was called 'One BBC: Making it Happen', to highlight that he was seeking more collaboration throughout the organization. Executive committee meetings were increasingly devoted to themes that cut across divisions, and members discovered areas in which they could combine forces to tackle new business opportunities.

In Tatum, New Mexico, the superintendent of schools organized five cross-cutting committees to challenge the fact that, even in a small town, people tended to talk to only a few people who tended to reinforce their current views. This invitational approach was centred on five aspects of community that would need to be addressed if the school-led community revitalization was to succeed. The five committees are focused on people, places, programmes, processes and policies. Out of a community of 600 people, 93 are actively involved in one of these interdependent committees.

When trying to increase collaboration, rather than continually reorganizing, smart leaders simply augment the organization chart with flexible, often temporary, groups that open relationships in multiple directions or bring together constituents from the school and community that seldom talk to one another. The task is to structure the organization, group or community to get the right discussions.

Communities learn differently from schools. Communities educate differently from schools. The attempt to build a learning community within a school causes confusion about school goals, and the roles various people can and should play in reaching those goals. This confusion can be a positive circumstance for transforming the school and the surrounding community in ways that can support and sustain learning throughout the community that results in healthier, happier, more productive, playful and creative citizens than we currently witness with the present arrangements.

Carl Moore, a retired professor at Kent State University, who now lives in Santa Fe, New Mexico, has helped groups build learning communities working with small schools and large cities. The authors have talked with Moore about helping people understand the confusion that results when institutions, such as schools, try to build a learning community by sharing a chart which compares the nature of community and institutional approaches to change and learning, as shown in Table 4.2.

Table 4.2 Community and institutional approaches to change

Communities learn by	Schools (managed institutions) learn by
Result of people acting through consent	Designed to create control of people
Recognition of fallibility	Assume things can be done right
Capacity to respond quickly	Have to involve all interests before acting
Encourage creative solutions	Require creative ideas to follow channels
Relationships are individualized	Hard to recognize unique characteristics of each individual
Care	Service
Depend upon capacity	Depend upon commodity deficiencies
Collective effort	Professional knowledge
Informality	Managed experiences/relationships
Knows it by stories	Know it by studies, reports
Celebrates: laughter, singing	Silence of long halls and reasoned meetings
Common knowledge of tragedy, death and suffering	No space for tragedy

Table 4.2 will help those who are building a learning community within schools to understand better where conflict can and will occur between learning in community and learning in a managed institution. The challenge we face today is building learning communities that integrate these two approaches to learning.

Community-based learning depends upon ways of relating that have served humanity for thousands of years. We suggest four that are essential to developing education as a shared function of both the school and the community. These are storytelling, play, games and dialogue. (Dialogue is the focus of Chapter 6.) These natural pedagogies are apparent in learning relationships throughout our communities. Storytelling allows young and old to connect, and passes on the traditions, values and morals of the culture and/or society in which we live. Play is nature's way of learning and productive learning in any conceivable human context is enhanced and improved when we play. Games are structured interactions, where people again learn the knowledge, skills and attitudes they need to accomplish almost any task. Playing games is also personally and socially satisfying, making us feel good to have friends, family and other associations where we can learn together. The importance of games in community learning is documented in the meteoric rise of the popularity of computer video games, a market segment that now outstrips both movies and music in terms of dollars spent in that sector.

Recently, schools have begun to understand the power of learning in these ways. Schools are beginning to introduce and integrate these natural pedagogies into the curriculum. Most school systems have been created specifically to train youth in the arts and sciences; we have become too dependent upon a pedagogy of memorization. There is now a movement to reintroduce these community learning methods back into the school experience, both before, during and after school.

Community-based approaches to teaching and learning are being swiftly adopted into the curriculum, activities and structure of schools. These approaches are being embraced even faster when families, schools and communities are working together. Mentoring, apprenticeships, civic involvement, service learning and community service are just a few of the strategies for teaching and learning that have always been part of learning in our communities that are being adopted by schools.

A recently released report from the US Coalition of Community Schools states the need for and shift towards community-based learning this way:

> In recent years, national tragedies – both manmade and natural – have forced Americans to see how much we rely on strong neighborhoods, communities, and democratic institutions. We've seen how lack of attention to their well being affects us all. These events lay bare the moral imperative that underlies the mission of public education – to develop active, engaged citizens who are able to participate in and contribute fully to a democratic society.
>
> In order to learn how to be citizens, students must act as citizens. Therefore, education must connect subject matter with the places where students live and the issues that affect us all. Schools are ideally situated to connect learning with real life; but typically, they do not. To a large extent, public education – following the lead of higher education – has failed to recognize the benefits of student engagement with their communities in acquiring knowledge. (Blank et al., 2006, page 1)

While community-based learning may look different depending on the school and community involved, there are a number of insights and understandings that are creating new learning communities between schools and communities, driving successful implementation of community-based learning initiatives, developing community leadership and promoting broad public support for lifelong learning for all.

None of us is as strong as all of us. We need each other more than we think if we are to provide the educational opportunities we all need to survive and thrive in today's world.

Community after community, from local to national, realize that society as a whole – families, community members, government, business, religion and students themselves, *along with the schools* – shares the responsibility for educating every citizen.

Schools belong to communities. Schools do not stand alone or apart. The school is and always has been an expression of the community in which it resides. Dissolving the myths of professionalism and autonomy that schools in our society have constructed are laying the ground for the establishment of learning communities where education is a shared function of everyone in the community and the school is a unique expression of how each community learns.

Families are the first and most important teachers. We know how interdependent educational access and opportunity are in modern nation states and how our over-reliance on schools to provide education ironically endangers our future. Regardless of the pressures on families to survive economically in modern societies, parents still recognize and, where possible, defend their role as teacher.

We all learn best by doing. Meeting after meeting between schools and members from the community, and the persistent plea of students themselves, indicate that learning by doing is and always will be the best way to acquire new knowledge, skill and behaviour. Much is known about how young people and adults learn and what motivates their interest. A considerable gap exists between what we intuitively know; what educational research has discovered; and the approach to teaching and learning employed by a majority of schools and educators. School leaders, parents, community members and students themselves understand that learning in today's world requires that community-based learning be available to everyone in the school and community.

In learning, positive, caring relationships matter most. Survey after survey indicate that a caring and knowledgeable teacher can keep a young person in school. A research study in South Australia, titled *Listen to Me, I'm Learning* (Smith et al., 2000), put it this way: 'how one or two negative teacher relationships can destroy school life; and how one positive teacher relationship can help a student remain at school' (page 294). You may not remember the history you studied but you will remember whether you liked it. You may not remember how to solve quadratic equations but you will remember whether the teacher cared about you, encouraged you and helped you to learn.

Building learning communities that are based on these new understandings will require different strategies for working together. We will have to focus more on building community and strengthening relationships. We will need strategies that utilize the natural pedagogies of storytelling, play, games and dialogue, and the methods of community-based learning to form working relationships between families, schools and communities that are capable of meeting the educational interests and needs of most if not all citizens.

5 Engaging families and the community

Introduction

If you have come to help me, you are wasting your time. But if you have come because your liberation is bound up with mine, then let us work together. (Lily Watson, Aboriginal Activist Sister)

We are clearly advocating the need to build learning communities that integrate and distribute educational provision among all stakeholders, because everyone has a stake in creating and implementing educational experiences that meet the interests and needs first for children and young people and then for all citizens. Yet, schools are no longer an integral part of the community. Therefore schools cannot only be about the business of improving themselves; they also need to address this isolation and alienation. Schools must transform their relationship with the community and families. According to complex systems theory, schools, like other human living systems, survive, develop and transform by experiencing, owning and integrating differences. This is accomplished by bringing together a diverse set of stakeholders to discover common ground through democratic processes, thereby developing social capital and reconnecting schools, families and communities. This chapter explains the practicality of linking schools and their key stakeholders to accomplish this new goal, and gives examples of the strategies, methods and processes that build these community-driven integrated learning communities. This chapter will explore:

- The need to engage with families and communities
- The challenge for schools
- Learning from others – examples of practice
- Principles for engaging with families and communities.

The need to engage with families and communities

In Chapters 1 and 2 the case was made for social context and place affecting children's achievement, but there is an increasing awareness of the impact of parents. Charles Desforges' (2003) definitive research on this subject has caused significant interest because of its core message that parents do make a difference to children's achievement levels, irrespective of family size or social class. He suggests that parental engagement can account for up to 12 per cent of the differences between various pupils' outcomes.

The statistics are thought provoking when the effect of parents is looked at alongside the effect of schools, as shown in Table 5.1.

Table 5.1 Effects of parents/effects of schools

Achievement	Parent/school effect
Age 7	0.29/0.05
Age 11	0.27/0.21
Age 16	0.14/0.51

Source: Desforges (2003)

In exploring exactly what parents *did* that made the difference, two factors had the most significant effect: high aspirations, and the quality of conversation and discussion in the home. This had a greater effect than parental engagement in school-based learning at home or the level of contact they had with the school. In other words this 'at-home good parenting' has a significant positive effect on children's achievement, even after all other factors affecting attainment have been taken into account. Differences between parents can be explained more by parental perceptions of their role, and their levels of confidence in fulfilling it, rather than primarily by their socio-economic status. Additional work by the OECD (Organization for Economic Co-operation and Development) and reported in the PISA study (2000) estimates that family social background accounts for 29 per cent of variation in student achievement.

The current policy environment has put parental involvement at its heart. Schools are being urged to reach out and involve parents whether it is through the provision of family learning events, the signing of home school contracts or, more punitively, through holding parents to account for their children's attendance at school.

The *Every Child Matters* core offer that all schools will be expected to provide in 2010, outlined in the DfES (2005b) extended schools prospectus, includes opening up the school facilities to the family and wider community and to offering parenting classes:

> Schools will want to work closely with parents to shape these activities around the needs of their community and may choose to provide extra services in response to parental demand. (DfES, 2005b, page 8)

And:

> The best schools know that they must work with others – with existing services and the voluntary sector but particularly with parents. It is vital that we ensure that the services are shaped by those who will use and provide them. (DfES, 2005b, page 4)

Excellence and enjoyment, the government's strategy for primary education (DfES, 2003), is clear on the need for parental partnership and the importance of this being developed locally in order that it meets local need. The importance of focusing on transition periods, when children and parents are particularly vulnerable, is highlighted, as is support for parents in helping their children to learn through family learning and support for parenting skills. It is also made clear that 'parents have responsibilities too' for ensuring their children attend school regularly and behave well.

There is also an acknowledgement that once children leave the Early Years stage of learning and care, levels of parental enagegement begin to drop. There is evidence that some parents believe that once children go to school, it is mainly the school's job to educate them. *Excellence and Enjoyment* (DfES, 2003) reports:

> Around 23% of parents said they believed it was 'mainly the school's responsibility' rather than being 'mainly the parents' responsibility', or 'a shared responsibility'. (page 52)

But policy documents can only go so far in promoting effective school/parent engagement. Too often, these policies look and feel like a one-sided conversation – one that appears to be conducted exclusively on the schools' terms. There is no wonder that many schools still talk about parents as the 'hard to reach'. From where the parents are standing the school is 'hard to reach'. For far too many parents their engagement with the school feels:

- as if it is led and instigated by the school;
- as if the problem lies with the parents;
- as if the school thinks it has the answers and believes it knows what parents want;
- as if the parents are classed primarily as helpers rather than co-educators.

Schools have struggled with their role in education for much of the last half-century. Find a new purpose for education in a changing society and sooner or later the school is expected to serve that purpose. Our demands on schools are immense. Even when research demonstrates conclusively that the school has little or no effect on a particular educational purpose, the school and its teachers are blamed for failing our young people once again. Teachers are pulled to and fro, trying to be mother, father, counsellor, doctor, friend, coach and spiritual adviser as well as teacher. Confusion reigns. Even in today's climate of teaching to the test and pushing academic performance as the clear purpose of schooling, the debate rages within schools and local communities as to how and where other crucial educational purposes will be addressed.

In the 1970s in Albuquerque, New Mexico, local community members were asked to rank order the many purposes of education that appeared in policy documents and school district vision statements. Hundreds of parents were surveyed and the results were enlightening. Parents wanted the schools to do everything. Over the years, schools have had to become more focused in their educational offerings, with providing general academic knowledge (focused on reading and maths) and providing knowledge-specific college preparation now clearly established as the two most important tasks of schooling. This trend has been increasingly embedded in state and federal policy statements and in funding priorities, and reached a zenith with the bipartisan support and passage of the No Child Left Behind Act in 2001.

A head-to-head debate on the question 'Is there a place for parents in schools?' (NCSL, 2005a) outlined polarized points of view. In one, a headteacher advocated strongly for parental engagement, in the other a converse view was expressed.

In one, the school's aim of 'being the best we can be' was not achievable without parental involvement. This was done through engaging parent governors, the Parents' and Friends' Association (PFA), and parent volunteers in the life of the school. Community classes were on offer and parents had work experience opportunities and employment placement in the school. The school began cautiously, but sees the value in being an 'open school' and in the obvious happiness children express when parents are in school.

The converse view was expressed by another headteacher who drew on the notion of expertise. His stance was that teachers are experts on learning and teaching, and an equal partnership with parents is impossible. The school fears that parents are increasingly abdicating their responsibilities of bringing up their children and use the school as a substitute, then question its professional judgement.

One school believes that learning together is the future, the other wants to be left alone to 'get on with it'.

The challenge for schools

If we are to engage in authentic partnerships that are mutually respectful, a change of stance is needed. Across the public sector there is a growing understanding of the need to involve the public in the ownership of the service. This requires the services themselves to be more 'customer focused'. A suite of leadership materials developed by the Cabinet Office on customer-focused leadership define it as:

> Customer focus is about public services treating users with dignity and respect, and ensuring that the services they receive represent value for money. (Cabinet Office, 2006)

This means seeing your service through the eyes of the customers, walking in their shoes and asking questions that genuinely enable you to understand how the school as an organization is perceived. It may mean taking risks in responding to customers. If we get this right then staff in schools will feel a greater sense of satisfaction as they engage with their core purpose, and customers (children, parents and families) will become more aware of what they can expect and will take a more proactive role. Taken to its most logical extent, an empowered client group, who are able to voice their needs, will begin to push up quality in the service they demand.

Schools are part of a community. Education is a community responsibility. Community education is what schools working with the community do to provide programmes, opportunities and structures for learning. Community education provides local residents and community agencies and institutions with the opportunity to become active partners in addressing community concerns and the educational needs of citizens. It is based on the following principles developed by Decker & Associates (1990):

> *Self-determination*: local people are in the best position to identify community needs and wants. Parents, as children's first and most important educators, have both a right and a responsibility to be involved in their children's education.
>
> *Self-help*: people are best served when their capacity to help themselves is encouraged and enhanced. When people assume ever-increasing responsibility for their own well-being, they acquire independence rather than dependence.
>
> *Leadership development*: the identification, development and use of the leadership capacities of local citizens are prerequisites for ongoing self-help and community improvement strategies.
>
> *Localization*: services, programmes, events and other community involvement opportunities that are brought closest to where people live have the greatest potential for a high level of public participation. Whenever possible, these activities should be decentralized to locations of easy public access.

Integrated delivery of services: organizations and agencies that operate for the public good can use their limited resources, meet their own goals and better serve the public by establishing close working relationships with other organizations and agencies with related purposes.

Maximum use of resources: physical, financial and human resources of every community should be interconnected and used to their fullest if the diverse needs and interests of the community are to be met.

Inclusiveness: the segregation or isolation of people by age, income, sex, race, ethnicity, religion or other factors inhibits the full development of the community. Community programmes, activities and services should involve the broadest possible cross-section of community residents.

Responsiveness: public institutions have a responsibility to develop programmes and services that respond to the continually changing needs and interests of their constituents.

Lifelong learning: learning begins at birth and continues until death. Formal and informal learning opportunities should be available to residents of all ages in a wide variety of community settings. (page 7)

This means being willing to address the issues of power and control, and access and openness that govern many schools. In looking at parental partnerships from an international perspective, Moss et al. (1999) questioned:

At one level this concerns 'openness', how easy is it for parents to approach and enter the school in the course of its normal operation? At another level this concerns power and rights. On what basis do children and parents use services – by universal entitlement or because they are deemed to be 'in need'? What real power do parents and children have over decision making? (page 37)

As schools engage with parents, some are finding out that 'animating the community' is an important part of the process. A study on community/school engagement commissioned by the NCSL from DEMOS (Craig and Skidmore, 2005) picks up two interesting examples. In one school, the generation of waiting lists for activities was enough to stimulate interest and engagement, and, in another, charging a nominal sum for activities stimulated participation:

These headteachers have learned that participation can be fickle and communities need to be animated as much as they need to be satisfied. (Craig and Skidmore, 2005, page 11)

For others, simple human contact can make the difference. One headteacher from Bournemouth describes meeting and greeting children and parents in the morning, outside the building; this helped break down many of the cultural barriers between herself, as a headteacher, and them as parents.

Suddenly there was far less angry shouting in my office and lots more simple conversations with parents. (Craig and O'Leary, 2005, page 14)

'Conversations in a box', is used to describe an innovation at Kingswood College of Arts, in Hull. The staff has developed a broadband community television project using set-top boxes in the home. These boxes initially focused on students' work, but have expanded to teachers filming their lessons and making them available. The school is just beginning to realize the potential of the project for parental engagement.

By focusing the pupils' homework on the television, they had created conversations in the home about learning. They realised that parents were using the channel to display a more active role in their children's learning and have increasingly tailored the content to meet parent's needs too. (Craig and O'Leary, 2005, page 15)

Others have found low-tech ways of generating the 'conversation in the box', by, for example, sending children home with seeds, encouraging them to grow herbs and get involved in family cooking. In Sefton, the fire service gives out smoke alarms to young pupils to give to their grandparents and to older members of the community. As Craig and O'Leary observe:

While some parents may be considered hard to reach from the perspective of the school, they are often not for the children, who live in the same house as them and talk to them every day. (page 15)

For some schools, finding a partner who can broker that relationship with parents has been the key to success:

You have to accept that you can't do things 'for' the community, you have to be equal partners. You have to find out what they want and what they can do for you. So, our local women's centre uses some of our facilities and has tapped into our expertise in fund raising and bid preparation. For us, they're a way into the local estate where many of our pupils live. The women have a real grasp of what services and facilities are needed there and they've helped us to get to know some of the very young parents. (NCSL, 2006b, page 15)

For others, responding to the expressed needs of the parents rather than the school has helped to build bridges:

We feel that we play the role of facilitator in the community and help to make things happen. Parents have set up an evening games club because there is nowhere for the children to play on the estates. We helped them to establish a constitution and paid for the insurance for the group but they actually run it themselves. (NCSL, 2006b, page 26)

Others describe the trust that builds up over time. A special school headteacher describes his close relationship with parents, and his knowledge that this was no guarantee that parents were going to use what the school 'put on' for them:

> Some of the things we have offered haven't worked. They came to one session but didn't return. We had said 'this is our policy and we want you to be part of it' but they were not keen. It works far better, we have found, when we say, 'what can we do for you?' It is hard to do sometimes but you really do have to go from where the parents are. (NCSL, 2006b, page 29)

It is clear from these examples that engagement with parents requires schools to think and behave differently: to think innovatively and deliberately try out something different. For many it is a trial and error approach; for all it is an ongoing conversation. For most it is something that cannot be planned but emerges through the developing relationship.

Schools can be hubs and facilitators of community learning. Schools are, in many instances, the natural place for community learning to occur. Sue Goodwin, a school administrator from Melbourne, Australia, found a way to integrate community, family and school needs. As a school leader she understood that the school's success was closely tied to the success of families and the surrounding community. Seeing the potential for increasing educational capacity throughout Port Phillip (a suburb of Melbourne), she linked with local council staff and members, the local police and young people development agencies, as well as all schools in the area, to explore ways to link schools and the community effectively. Using the principles of community education as a framework for discussion, Sue went to local council meetings, talked with police about their resources, and interviewed students, teachers, parents and community leaders. Then she brought representatives from these interested groups together to plan what they could all do to improve education. The result is the 'Community School Yard', an initiative that belongs equally to all sectors of the community and is managed by a steering committee made up of representatives from all the organizations mentioned. Finding ways to link the school with the community depends on:

- identifying new roles and purposes for working together on educational issues;
- focusing on strengths not weaknesses;
- keeping people engaged with each other;
- paying attention to the dynamic of bonding and bridging;
- schools and local communities moving into high levels of social capital;
- the realization of and tapping into interdependence.

The key is to involve everybody.

Learning from others – examples of practice

Charles Desforges (2003) makes an interesting analogy in his research. He likens the knowledge we have about the need for parental involvement, and how to put it into practice, to Newton's work on the physics of motion in the seventeenth century:

> By 1650 Newton knew in theory how to put a missile on the moon. It took more than 300 years to learn how to do this in practice. The scientists who did this used Newton's physics with modern engineering knowledge. We must not wait 300 years to promote stellar advances in pupils' achievement. We need urgently to learn how to apply the knowledge we already have in the field. (Desforges, 2003, page 90)

We know, in theory, how to engage parents and schools in powerful partnerships – but we don't yet put this into practice consistently or deeply enough. What examples can we take from the field to help us in the application of our knowledge?

The Swedish government's Committee on Child Care extols the power of the developmental conversation. This involves the teacher, parent and child engaging together in a structured conversation on an equal level.

The Swedish Committee on Child Care states:

> One objection to more parental influence in the school was that parents lack competence to participate in decision making concerning the central issues in the school. We maintain that parents, in order to take part in school life, do not need any other competence than the one they already possess as parents, professionals and citizens. What parents can supply above all is knowledge about their own children. Furthermore parents can share their experiences from work life, from local society and from the spare time activities of the children. Parents' lack of knowledge about school is a passing phenomenon. By and by they will, through participating in work in school, learn much about school and the conditions of the school. (Moss et al., 1999, page 31)

Part of the Swedish enactment of this commitment is the 'developmental conversation' which takes place between the parent, the educator and the child, and operates with a clear set of principles.

The 'Share' project in the UK is designed to promote family learning that is closely linked to everyday life and situations, to stimulate parents and children learning together. It aims to demonstrate the need to address issues of purpose, engagement, motivation, learning and accreditation and organizational structures when engaging with parents. Its aims are to:

- improve the educational attainment and achievement of children;
- motivate parents to take an active interest in their children's education;

- increase parents' understanding of the vital role they play in their children's learning;
- enable parents to gain accreditation for what they learn as they support their children's learning;
- develop effective management and organization of parental involvement in schools/settings. (ContinYou.org.uk, 2006)

A Reception teacher engaged in the scheme is clear of the benefits to children:

> It's an added bonus to work with their parents in school – it's time spent with the children on a 1–1 basis … It helps build confidence in children at school, as they feel valued in what they are achieving. (DfES, 2003)

And for parents:

> Share Family Learning helps them understand where their children are, and therefore what their needs are. It helps build their own confidence because they are able to help each other and gain ideas along the way. We often find that the adults soon feel enabled to start thinking about continuing their own education. (DfES, 2003)

As in Sweden, in the Early Years community in the UK it has long been understood that parents have a critical role as a child's primary educator, and that parents and families are equal partners in the education process. This development of an equal and active partnership between nursery and home, early childhood educator and parent, is increasingly embedded in Early Years practice and has much to teach the rest of the system.

Dr Margy Whalley (2002), at the Pen Green Leadership and Research Base, talks about a 'triangle of care' which describes a new kind of partnership between child, parent and early childhood educator. In 1995, Margy and her colleagues took the step to formalize their research work in a way that involved parents and children as co-partners in it. In order to do this a shared code of ethics was developed:

- Be positive for all participants.
- Provide data that are open to, accountable to and interpreted by all the participants.
- Focus on the questions that the participants themselves (parents, children and staff) are asking.
- Be based on a position of trust where people's answers are believed.
- Produce results that are about improving practice at home and at nursery.

The leadership questions that informed this research are worth noting here, and may be of use as a starting point for enquiry in your own setting:

1. What is the real impact of parental involvement on children's learning?
2. How important is the role of parents as well-informed advocates to their children's progress at school?
3. How can parents' insights into their children's learning inform curriculum planning?
4. What kind of impact does this dialogue have on parents working and playing with their children at home?
5. How can this kind of genuine partnership be sustained into primary and secondary schools?
6. How have you been able to encourage staff to develop an equal and active relationship with parents where information can be shared? (Whalley, 2002, page 14)

In East Manchester, education is at the heart of the regeneration process and engaging parents is the key to its success. Their VIP (very important parent) days, which celebrate parents in East Manchester, are held at a non-school venue and involve stalls, workshops and activities. This and other initiatives have begun to make east Manchester a place of high aspiration for others to attain to. As Julia Duffy, who co-ordinates the work, observes:

> Pupils, adults, families, school members – all people involved in the endeavour of East Manchester now have higher aspirations and a greater collective, concerted effort to reach them. (2005, page 7)

The Effective Partnerships with Parents Association – the EPPA network – began in 1998 and was set up to help define what effective and productive partnerships with parents mean in practice in Plymouth, Torbay and Devon. The partnership is based on the belief that an informed and supportive parent body will be best placed to support the school in its ambition to raise standards.

The EPPA strategy has much to teach us, as it is parent led and works through parent action teams. This means that it is the parents, not the teachers or the governors, who take the responsibility for its success. It is interesting to note that:

> In the pilot, parent action teams that were reliant on headteachers to lead were unsustainable. When parents led, more was achieved; community and parents were more engaged and empowered. However, senior leaders in schools must also be involved. Without the headteacher or other senior management participation, action teams lost the school perspective and did not thrive. (de Rijke, 2005, page 3)

In addition, by moving outside the school domain, parent-led action teams were more easily able to recruit support and resources from the wider community to help the work to be sustainable.

In Highfield Primary School, one parent action team raised funds to convert an unused space in the school and turn it into a 'halfway house' between the school and the community. This is now a thriving space used by the school and the community for breakfast and after-school clubs and other school/community focused events. This action has set up a virtual circle in which a broad range of people has benefited:

- Pupils benefit by using the facility and by belonging to families engaged with school.
- Teachers and pupils benefit through the improved behaviour and concentration of children in class following the breakfast club.
- Parent action team members have received training in health and safety, ICT, first aid and food hygiene.
- Many of the action team parents have subsequently become valued members of the school staff as learning support assistants, thus further developing their skills and providing employment.

One headteacher provided valuable advice when he urged others to 'not give up', even though in his area the group started very slowly. He commented:

> Parent leadership is essential. I hear their ideas instead of setting an agenda and guessing what parents want. (De Rijke, 2005, page 4)

In the Sandwell area of the West Midlands, family learning networks have been set up where parents are empowered to support their children's learning and through this develop their own learning. Each network is supported by a town learning co-ordinator, a learning champion and an e-learning mentor.

This has led to parents meeting regularly with other parents to support each other in their family learning. 'Families engaging with schools' has now become a core part of the Sandwell Teacher of the Future programme. In Sandwell, the importance of keeping the networks local and led by someone local and known to the residents of the area (the town learning co-ordinator) is important. Finding new ways of recording information was also key to the success of the project, and photographic and video evidence has been assembled, while those involved in the programme are encouraged to keep a learning journal.

Because traditional methods of involving parents and community had so clearly failed in the Santa Fe Schools in New Mexico, work began with the Center for RelationaLearning to design an approach to interacting with parents and the community that would develop and build social capital as a primary goal of the community involvement strategy. The project centres on 'public conversations' involving common interest groups (for example, all parents or all teachers) who are trained in public conversation skills. Once confidence has developed and their voice is strong, they then move into mixed interest groups. The project is designed to:

- enhance deliberative and civic skills;
- promote community involvement in education and collaborative problem solving;
- focus on teaching and learning;
- generate a new understanding of and commitment to education;
- use public conversations as a means to improve education.

Dialogue in these settings is seen as having a number of positive attributes: it creates positive and sophisticated networks; enhances the communication skills in the community; and can help secure involvement and sustain motivation. The conversations about education are, of themselves, educative. The process is also fundamentally democratic in that it encourages participation and builds capability in communities that have been traditionally disenfranchized.

Power and responsibility

The think tank, DEMOS, has been actively engaged in exploring new forms of schooling and parental engagement. It argues that if parents are to become active participants in the educational process, then this needs to be formalized, and some power and responsibility needs to be devolved. A recent report (Craig and Perri 6, 2004) argues that while today the talk is of *extending* schools, the real challenge is to *shrink* them, empowering other agencies and communities to treat the school as a public resource. The report suggests that, to achieve this, community involvement will be vital. It argues that 1 per cent of a school's budget should be distributed among its parents in the form of 'voice vouchers', enabling them to make collective decisions about spending priorities for the coming year:

> Voice vouchers would drive the involvement of parents in school decisions, and schools to capitalise on the social capital that they help to build. (Craig and Perri 6, 2004, page 59)

Principles for engaging with families and communities

Characteristics of effective practice

It appears that we are very slowly moving from a system characterized by the school having 'power over' the parent, to the school and parent having 'power with' each other. At least we know the 'power over' model, characterized by traditional approaches to consultation, is not working. The best parent/school partnership projects are characterized by the following:

- Parents and school as equal partners.

- Parents as a resource – not as a problem.

- Doing with, not doing to.

- Led by parents, supported by school.

Guiding principles to changing practice

Small steps get us started on this path, and the following appear to be good guiding principles to help us take these first steps:

- Seek out the wisdom and leadership of parents and others.

- Build a culture of conversation.

- Think and start small – small intimate groups work best. Encourage the emergence of natural leadership in these groups. Work hard to make people feel special.

- Be prepared for things to go differently from what you expect and also for conflict. Parents may not immediately want to concentrate on school matters.

- Understand that conflict and struggle mean that people are being honest.

Charles Desforges (2003, page 87), in the conclusion to his research, suggests that the following principles should guide any action:

- collaboration should be proactive rather than reactive;

- the engagement of all parents should be worked for;

- collaboration involves sensitivity to the wide-ranging circumstances of all families;

- collaboration recognizes and values the contributions parents have to make to the educational process.

So what can we do?

There are many small steps schools can take – some starting points might be:

- Look at the external environment – is the main entrance well signposted and welcoming? 'Visitors and parents must report to the main office' – could be changed to: 'We welcome visitors, parents and carers, please come to the main office so we can help you.'

- Is there a procedure for ensuring that all written and telephone enquiries from parents are dealt with promptly, and is there a way of monitoring that?

- What forms of communication with parents do you encourage, for example informal meeting and greeting at the school gates, telephone contact and home visits?

- Are parents contacted for positive as well as negative reasons – do the positive reasons outnumber the negative?

- Should consideration be given to the use of 'mail merge' to personalize some letters to parents?

- Do signatures on letters to parents include forenames?

- Does the school encourage the use of parents as volunteers and is there a strategy, through remodelling, to employ parents and provide them with opportunities for training and development?

- If a parent has a good idea, how easy is it for him or her to find someone to talk about it to?

- Is value placed on all parents, irrespective of background or ability, and how would parents recognize this?

(Adapted from Better Together seminar discussions)

6 Dialogue as a community resource

Real change begins with the simple act of people talking about what they care about. It only takes two or three friends to notice that they're concerned about the same thing – and then the world begins to change. Their first conversation spreads. Friends talk to friends. Because friends care about each other, they pay attention to what is being said. Then they talk to others and it grows and grows. (Wheatley, 2002, page 22)

Dialogue – from the Greek *dia logos*, the flow of meaning through or among us – is one of the most natural methods for learning in a community. In most contemporary teaching and learning relationships it has become a lost art. In this chapter, we revisit the practice and indicate ways to utilize this essential methodology for learning in a community.

This chapter explores the centrality of dialogue to all social interactions and focuses on how it can help build social capital and enable learning. The chapter offers models of effective practice and shows how dialogue can be incorporated into community and educational activities. The chapter focuses on:

- The role of dialogue in community learning
- The three conversations and dialogue
- Conditions that promote dialogue
- Building conversational capacity.

The role of dialogue in community learning

Learning in community is fuelled by dialogue. Participation in dialogue is the surest way to build social capital. Community education is, in essence, the continuing dialogue we have with each other about who we are, what is worth learning, and how we can acquire that knowledge, skill or attitude individually and collectively. Participation in dialogue helps to create a sense of community. Dialogue, over time, promotes the shared creation of meaning and understanding within the community. Dialogue informs the movement to individual and collective action that increases educational opportunity for everyone.

Dialogue is both the medium and message in human learning. In the best sense, in dialogue we dance with each other. Dance is the physical embodiment of our highest aspirations and our most enduring hopes. Whatever form it takes, dance is an irresistible impulse. To dance is to trace the intricate patterns of our lives, to convey the breadth of feeling that makes us who we are. It is the acting out of joyful memories, the communicating through vivid movements of our most poignant circumstances. Meticulously planned or spontaneously transmitted, dance expresses an important part of our lived condition – both individual and shared.

As anyone knows who has tried it, dance is freeing and life-enhancing, but it can also be challenging. In many cultures we learn to dance much the same way we learn to walk, talk and eat. Like the air we breathe, we dance. Yet, in other cultures, to dance well requires repeated trials. Regular and persistent practice is a must.

Dance can be an art in which we may express our deepest longings. But it is also a discipline and a craft that improves the more often we attempt it. Dance can be either simple or highly complex. Either way, dance satisfies. But dancers have more choices, more creative directions in which to push their art when they learn and master a variety of moves, when they acquire a broad repertoire of positions, steps and styles. Like any art or craft, dance is a discipline that grows richer and more varied through effort and experimentation.

Dance teems with life. It is an act of creating something together that demands each person's full and concentrated participation. It is the embodiment of human mutuality, a fulfilment of the teaming concept. It is most of all an affirmation of life and the physical expression of the broadest range of human experiences.

Everything that has just been stated about dance the authors think can also be said about dialogue. Dialogue, too, is life. It, too, reflects our commitment to collaboration and making the most of our conversational partners. Dialogue, too, is an art and a discipline that deepens and grows more meaningful the more we engage in it. Dialogue also gets better the more we try out different 'moves' and experiment with a variety of ways to listen more fully, speak more fluently from the heart, communicate more coherently, affirm others more generously and learn more lastingly from those around us.

It has been said that dance is a universal, supremely human endeavour. The authors make the same claim for dialogue. Without it, we are greatly diminished. But with dialogue in our daily lives, the opportunities for learning, growth, community development, even for lasting peace, are tremendously increased.

In a sentence, the role of dialogue in community learning is to connect us to each other and help each of us to express that enduring longing, that nagging sense that we want to feel and be more connected to our neighbours, next door and around the world.

Learning is one of the things that most sharply defines us as human beings. It makes us feel more vital and alert, and lends meaning to the simplest of actions and the most modest of thoughts. It reminds us of our nearly unlimited capacity for growth, on the one hand, and, on the other, of how partial and uncertain most of our knowledge actually is. A lifelong learner is an individual struggling for clarity and self-understanding, but is also a member in good standing of the community of learners. The quest for happiness depends on our being active participants in such a learning community, and on recognizing that most of the things worth knowing are learned through collaboration with other learners. We do not in the least underestimate the value of growing as an individual knower and learner, but we also affirm that learning is, at its highest and most complex levels, an interdependent process. And as an interdependent process, learning is most richly and excitingly and enduringly attained through dialogue.

Poetry, like dialogue and dance, is a form of making art and therefore signifies a learning situation where input and output models of production simply cannot speak to the mysteries of the creative process. The following poem speaks of the need for real dialogue in our communities using our dance metaphor.

Advice

Someone dancing inside us
learned only a few steps:
the 'Do-your-work' in 4/4 time,
the 'what do you expect' waltz.
He hasn't noticed yet the woman
standing away from the lamp,
the one with black eyes
who knows the rhombi,
and strange steps in jumpy rhythms
From the mountains in Bulgaria.
If they dance together,
something unexpected will happen.
If they don't, the next world
will be a lot like this one.

(Holm, 1990, page 54)

The three conversations and dialogue

The life-blood of education is conversation. We are always in a conversation when we are in a teaching and learning context. The nature of the conversation will determine the character of the learning. In schools we find ourselves in one of three conversations: instructional, discovery or community (as discussed below). Learning as a community requires that we spend more time in discovery and community conversations and less time in instructional conversations. Dialogue is the medium of exchange that makes a community conversation work. And dialogue produces more ownership, interest, energy and action than any other form of a discovery conversation. Dialogue will also improve an instructional conversation. You can have, as we often do, an instructional conversation without engaging in dialogue. A discovery conversation and dialogue share more similarities than differences, and a community conversation only becomes possible through dialogue.

Instructional conversation

This is the conversation we have most often in schools today. This is the one we see most often in the classroom. It is to do with a relationship in which our discussion is about acquiring skill, extra knowledge, perhaps career training – something external to ourselves – a skill or ability.

The vast majority of teaching and learning relationships expects that learning of most worth will be the result of explicit instruction. An instructional conversation is a very structured interaction with clear boundaries between student and teacher. The teacher, most often an adult, has knowledge, skill and attitudes that are to be transferred to the student, usually a child or young person. We depend on instructional conversations to teach the young what to think, how to act and what to believe. Most conversations in schools and school settings follow this model. I have information, knowledge or skill that you need or want and we set a time, place and method for that information, knowledge or skill to be transferred from one person to another. In a dramatic way, the instructional conversation sets up a dependency between the student and the teacher that demeans the student and gives false authority to the teacher. In most classrooms, the teacher stands while the students sit, the teacher talks and the students listen, the teacher presents and explains as the students record and try to memorize. The list of physical, social and psychological inequities that inform most instructional conversations in educational settings is truly mind-boggling, especially when an instructional conversation can be a mutually beneficial way of learning. Improving the quality of instructional conversations is currently a major focus for professional educators who know that getting the instructional conversation right will go a long way to improving educational provision for everyone involved in schooling as currently constituted.

There is a simple way to state the progression of an instructional conversation in a way that almost anyone can understand.

You do it

You do it, they watch

They do it, you watch

They do it, you correct

They do it.

Discovery conversation

The second conversation in which we can participate, and which we can open up to everyone, is a discovery conversation. A discovery conversation is closer to one in which our mutual growth is the end result. It matters greatly because it parallels dialogue, and dialogue is a conversation that you enter without knowing the outcome when you begin. In this conversation, relationship and task get equal attention.

Discovery conversations help everyone explore who they are, what is worth learning and how to learn what is needed or important or interesting. They are based upon several premises:

- Wisdom, knowledge, skills and ideas are widely distributed in communities.
- Everyone can be a student, teacher or leader where learning is concerned.
- Both structure and space for creativity are required to progress thinking and actions.
- Worthwhile learning relationships depend on a continuing exchange of ideas.

Recently, a national programme to redesign schools in the US used discovery conversations to their fullest and the results were nothing less than astounding. The discovery conversation was the heart of the *joinedupdesignforschools* programme. It was the period during which school teams and the designers, through a series of meetings, brainstorms and visits to inspiring places, forged a partnership by getting to know one another, sharing ideas and planning together. After designers, who had not worked with children before and had not been in a school for 30 years, got to know the children and the children got to know the designers, everyone got to work. The report of the project stated the power of, what is here called, discovery conversations this way:

> The conversation developed over several weeks, a number of the designers devising exciting brainstorming sessions, others creating workshops in which they generated ideas with the pupils through making models. The extensive length of the pupils' involvement with external professionals had several advantages. It allowed the pupils to get to know the designers really well, overcome their initial shyness and develop skills and learning through the gradual nature of the process. 'It's a different way of learning because you're

not just sitting there and getting stuff out of books,' said a fifteen-year-old boy from Tyneside. 'You're actually sitting there and giving your ideas.' (Sorrell and Sorrell, 2005, page 20)

Community conversation

The third and increasingly needed conversation for learning is a community conversation. A community conversation is a conversation where we make meaning, continually define ourselves as a learning community, more consciously discover who we are collectively, what we value, want and need educationaly, and how we might collaborate to act and learn in context. Community conversation is a vehicle for people to express and share the diverse views that they hold; to negotiate and reaffirm directions and vision; to develop social capital.

Better than anyone, Margaret Wheatley captures the power and purpose of a community conversation:

> I first fell in love with the practice of conversation when I experienced for myself the sense of unity, of communion, that is available in this process. Most of what we do in communities and organizations focuses us on our individual needs. We attend a conference or meeting for our own purposes, for 'what we can get out of this.'...
>
> Although we each benefit individually from good conversation, we also discover that we were never as separate as we thought. Good conversation connects us at a deeper level. As we share our different human experiences, we rediscover a sense of unity. We remember we are part of a greater whole. And as an added joy, we also discover our collective wisdom. We suddenly see how wise we can be together. (Wheatley, 2002, page 28)

Key stages of a community conversation are:

1. Connecting to each other.
2. Agenda negotiation.
3. Connecting to the issues at hand.
4. Exploration.
5. Insight.
6. Reflection.
7. Action, change and new agendas.
8. You know you are part of a community conversation when ...
9. You are more interested in being real rather than being good or right.
10. You notice that you are not feeling the need to get somewhere as a result of the conversation.

Facilitating dialogue

All three types of conversation are enhanced when dialogue is the medium of exchange, but community conversations especially depend on it. The importance of relationships – grounded in equitable, fair and respectful discourse – to the development of a culture of participation and learning, cannot be overemphasized.

Before one can facilitate dialogue, one must be clear about the characteristics of it and the conditions under which it operates in a conversation.

Characteristics of dialogue

The most important characteristic of dialogue is its open-ended nature. This characteristic is dialogue's foundation as stated by Nel Noddings, a professor of education at Stanford University:

> Dialogue is open-ended; that is, in a genuine dialogue, neither party knows at the outset what the outcome or decision will be. As parents and teachers, we cannot enter dialogue with children when we know that our decision is already made. It is maddening to young people (or any people) to engage in dialogue with a sweetly reasonable adult who cannot be persuaded and who, in the end, will say, 'Here's how it's going to be. I tried to reason with you …' We do have to talk this way at times, but we should not pretend that this is dialogue. (Noddings, 1992, page 23)

Open-endedness means that dialogue becomes more a search for understanding than for answers, and results in the development of empathy or appreciation more than explanations or solutions. At its core, dialogue is always a genuine quest for something undetermined at the beginning.

Dialogue builds a sense of community. It connects us to each other and helps maintain caring relationships. Through dialogue we come to know each other better, and we can serve each other's educational interests when we understand what others in our community need and the history of that need. By building up a substantial knowledge of one another through our conversations we can create educational opportunities that are personalized and productive for more and more citizens.

Conditions that promote dialogue

One set of conditions has to do with the attitudes or dispositions that participants should practise to create good dialogue. When we lead discussions, we try to get participants to be aware of these dispositions. We also model them and encourage participants to adopt these dispositions themselves. We can never expect more than partial success in acting on these dispositions, but even naming them and being aware of them helps participants to move towards more collaborative and respectful interactions. We have found the following to be especially relevant and useful:

1. hospitality
2. participation
3. mindfulness
4. humility
5. mutuality
6. deliberation
7. appreciation
8. hope
9. autonomy.

Hospitality

By hospitality we mean the sort of inviting, welcoming, engaging spirit that prevails in dialogue sessions where each person feels that his or her involvement is essential. Hospitality communicates to each participant, 'without you we are diminished: we are incomplete'. Additionally, hospitality implies that participants are attentive to the physical setting, to seating arrangements that encourage engagement, and to helping one another become comfortable together.

Participation

Although no one who joins a public gathering to discuss controversial issues should feel compelled to talk, participation from everyone helps the group learn. The facilitator should reinforce the notion that there are many ways to contribute to the conversation and that every person participates, even in silence, and that each person's participation has an impact on group deliberations.

Mindfulness

Dialogue cannot be as effective without individual and group mindfulness. It means paying attention at many different levels. We need to be mindful of what each person says, how it is said and how it relates to what has already been said. But we also must be mindful of what is not being said, of issues that are being avoided and of participants who are feeling silenced. Finally, we must pay attention to the arc of the entire discussion and note how well it is addressing the issues that the group has gathered to explore.

Humility

This often-mentioned disposition is a reminder that no one person's knowledge and understanding are total. When humility is practised, participants accept that there is always more to learn and that the group's collective wisdom benefits each individual.

In dialogue, humble participants listen at three levels – they listen to self, to others and they listen for the shared meaning.

Mutuality

This disposition suggests that the more each participant is free to contribute what she or he knows, the more everyone else profits. Mutuality says that when I allow other people the space to speak, when I give others the room to share their experience, I am also advantaged because I also expand my experiential horizons and deepen my understanding.

Deliberation

This notion goes to the heart of good dialogue. It refers to the willingness of participants to explore issues as fully as possible. In most educational settings we deliberate by offering arguments and counter-arguments supported by evidence, data and logic. Deliberation obliges us to formulate well-substantiated positions and to support our positions unless there are good reasons not to do so. When we embrace this condition for dialogue, the reasons we offer for the positions we take are primary. However, deliberation also requires us to remain alert to the reasons other participants put forward and to adopt them if they are sufficiently compelling and persuasive.

To be more inclusive our deliberations must make room for other ways of knowing how to enter the dialogue. For example, the people of Taos Pueblo have a deliberative tradition where a community concern can be discussed and resolved with no words being spoken in the deliberations. The power of experience and sense of community is explored and communicated non-verbally with resounding impact. We must be careful in our deliberation not to exclude feminine, intuitive and indigenous viewpoints as to what constitutes appropriate and relevant experience, evidence, data and logic.

Appreciation

This is one of the most neglected of dispositions. It calls on us to take the time to acknowledge a useful insight or an illuminating contribution. It implies that the opportunity to discuss difficult issues with others is wonderful and life-enhancing and that we should seize every chance to express our gratitude to others. When our participation in a dialogue is waning, and interest and energy are low, we suggest that the facilitator has participants take a short break from the discussion to share appreciations. This sharing quite often revitalizes the group and encourages further discussion.

Hope

In his *Pedagogy of Hope*, the late Paulo Freire (1994) mentions that he cannot comprehend human existence or the struggle to improve it without a foundation in hope. As difficult as educational reform and social change can be, hope must be one of the mainstays of good dialogue. Hope assumes that a great deal of good can emerge from people taking the time to gather together to talk about the important issues of the day. Most of all, hope affirms our collective capacity to use dialogue to envision new possibilities and to act on behalf of the common good.

Autonomy

This disposition reminds us of the responsibility to stand up for what we believe. Dialogue can never be used as a tactic to get people to believe or act in ways that lack personal integrity. Neither is dialogue useful if participants feel compelled to 'go along' with the group on a particular issue or approach. It does not negate in any way the value of learning from the group or from sometimes adopting the views of the group. It simply says that there are times when we must defy the collective deliberations of the group and go our own way, however contrary that may appear to others. It reinforces the idea that groups are strongest when the identities of individual members are given their due and when each person's passions and commitments are allowed a fair hearing.

Building conversational capacity

Broadening our understanding of dialogue and the many important ways we learn together (instructional, learning and community conversations) will increase all stakeholders' ability to improve and expand learning and educational opportunity in school and community. Everyone in a community dedicated to learning can promote and practise better conversations, and thereby develop more effective and satisfying teaching and learning relationships throughout the community.

Regardless of the particular kind of conversation we encounter, there are three aspects of a conversation that are worthy of our awareness and in which we can deliberately improve the experience of everyone involved.

How we enter

Strategies to consider when you bring people together include:

- Acknowledge people for attending.
- Acknowledge the importance of the meeting with ceremony, if possible.
- Setting clear rules or terms of engagement.
- Not forcing participation – be invitational in your approach.
- Search for and acknowledge common interest and experience.
- Help participants to be mentally present at the meeting and not somewhere else.
- Personalize the event by bringing in participants' stories and experience.
- Take time to get to know each other as people.

How we conduct

Strategies for conducting conversations and meetings include:

- Dialogue.
- Ensuring participation individually, in pairs, in small groups and in a full group.
- Conduct periodic check-in and feedback sessions.
- Use processes that allow everyone to say what they really feel and think.
- Lots of opportunity to question 'why' as well as 'how'.

How we conclude

Strategies for concluding conversations include:

- Thank you and acknowledgements.
- Appreciations.
- Create agenda for next session.
- Commitments.
- Celebrate successes, again, where possible, with ceremony.

Paying close attention to how participants are engaged from the beginning to the end of a conversation will enhance participation, create ownership and develop strong collaborative relationships within the school community. Before you facilitate a meeting or conversation you might attempt to develop some strategies for how you and the participants will enter, conduct and conclude their time together.

Engaging in dialogue around change

This simple format for dialogue among stakeholders can effectively tap social capital and yield new understandings, agreements and actions. Someone who understands the role of dialogue in community learning and can facilitate dialogue can help stakeholders build their conversational capacity using this simple format.

The dialogue is conducted in rounds. Each round can take one hour or more and ends with a short reflection period and the listing of critical questions for the next round. Rounds may follow each other after a short break or may take place over a number of days or even weeks. The point is that the conversation is ongoing. Also, participation in the dialogue does not require any specific action on any person's part. Participation in any round may and most often does result in individuals, small groups or the entire group deciding to act on what they are learning from each other in dialogue. There are many formats for such planning and agreement making. These actions are not a formal part of the dialogue, yet dialogue transforms each of us and leads to action. The template at the end of this chapter can be used as is or changed accordingly.

Remember that each round is a new event, that questions can be repeated and revised, and that the discussion really never ends. After several rounds, though, you may want to take a break, start with a fresh focus and begin the dialogue again. One of my favourite focus questions is, 'What does it take to become a healthy, happy, constructive adult?'

To gain a feel for how dialogue can develop in a mixed group of stakeholders, read *Socrates Café* by Christopher Phillips (2002), and for guidelines for discussion and support for the power of dialogue for learning in community read *Turning To One Another* by Margaret Wheatley (2002). A good source of activities that enhance dialogue can be found in *Skills for Democracy* by Stephen Preskill, George Otero and Lois Vermilya (2000). This book contains 15 practical strategies that will help everyone in the school and community develop conversational skills needed to create the learning communities we have discussed in this book.

The introduction states the value of dialogue to school transformation this way:

> Good dialogue encourages people to solve their problems collaboratively, to see one another as valuable sources of knowledge and experience, and to forge new links with each other. In our view, there is no surer route to community building and to fulfilling the promise of democracy and lifelong learning than through the deepening of good, on-going dialogue. Such dialogue can increase student achievement, transform teaching and learning and renew relationships that connect communities to their schools. (Preskill et al., 2000, page 4)

Finally, these signposts of a culture of dialogue will help stakeholders in the school and the community to know that relationships – grounded in equitable, fair and respectful discourse – are a community resource. Our capacity to learn from each other through democratic discourse, despite major differences in experience and viewpoint, can lead to decisive civic action that promotes educational attainment, social justice and mutual respect.

Signposts of a culture of dialogue

- We practise 'power-with', not 'power-over'.
- We care as much about questions as we care about answers.
- We grow comfortable with ambiguity, uncertainty, not-knowing and paradox.
- We strive to be as much as we strive to do.
- We care as much about the learning of others as we do about our own learning – indeed, individual learning and group learning are inseparable.
- We devote as much energy to listening as we do to speaking.
- We value the process of witnessing the thoughts and feelings of others as much as we appreciate individual opportunities for self-reflection and disclosure.
- We leave ourselves open to be changed by the conversation.

ENGAGING IN DIALOGUE AROUND CHANGE

Facilitated by _____

Date _____

You are invited to explore the following questions with colleagues, friends and neighbours. Share and enjoy!

Critical questions – Round 1

What changes are needed within us, our teachers and the wider community to establish, enhance and sustain the learning environments we are all trying to create?

What do our previous experiences with change tell us?

How do we maintain optimism for ourselves, support staff, parents and students through the shift?

What is social capital and what role does it play in the changes we are seeking?

What stories, experiences and ideas can we share that will support our understanding of leading change in chaotic times?

REFLECTION AND QUESTIONS FOR NEXT ROUND

Please take a few minutes to reflect on what you have said and heard. In twos or threes share your insights, feelings and experience. Now, what would you suggest might be a critical question for round 2?

Critical question – Round 2

7 From silos to services

The *Every Child Matters* agenda (DfES, 2005a) and its emphasis on joined-up services and extended schooling, challenges our old conception of schools and schooling. It requires schools to open themselves up to the world beyond the school gate. As they connect with agencies, professionals, parents and community members, extended schools will become places where people of all backgrounds can work together for the good of each child:

> An extended school is a school that recognises that it cannot work alone in helping children and young people to achieve their potential, and therefore decides to work in partnership with other agencies that have an interest in outcomes for children and young people, and with the local community. In doing so, it aims to help meet not only the school's objectives but also to share in helping to meet the wider needs of children, young people, families and their community. (DfES, 2005b])

For many schools, which have a long-established record of collaboration, this is an enhancement of their work. For others, it is a new and often challenging way of working. For all schools, the promotion of an open culture that embraces the ethos of partnership working and partner organizations is required.

This chapter explores the issues and tensions in moving from autonomous silos to integrated services. From 'vertical' freestanding provision to 'horizontal' integrated strategies. The chapter will review the following topics:

- Moving from silos to services
- What makes multi-agency partnerships successful?
- A new professionalism?

Moving from silos to services

It would be naïve to imagine that the move from silos to services will be easy to achieve. The silos of public-sector provision – education, social services, housing, health, police and so on – have almost 150 years of autonomy to 'unlearn'; it is a classic example of moving from bonding to bridging. For much of their history, the various public-sector agencies have been actively encouraged to develop distinctive professional identities. Much of this was under the cloak of professional status, whereby they developed:

- a unique professional culture;
- a distinctive vocabulary;
- career structure;
- protocols and working procedures;
- self-legitimating and self-reinforcing cultures.

In many ways this process was essential to the creation of a professional identity but, as was demonstrated in Chapter 2, eventually became a negative force, as the integrity of each silo's internal functioning detracted from the service it was intended to provide.

This problem is exemplified in Figure 7.1 which shows a 'cross-section' of the silos each providing a service, on its terms, with no reference to the other silos. The ideal – the movement from silos to services – is shown where the silos are integrated with the client.

The problems inherent in this transition are described by Lownsbrough and O'Leary (2005):

> Entrenched patterns of professional behaviour lead to scepticism and distrust of the capabilities of professionals from other backgrounds. The temptation to return to familiar habits in the face of major uncertainty can be powerful.
>
> In other words, changes to structure and policy that are intended to generate a transformation of working practices can too easily be neutralised by prevailing professional identities and behavioural norms. When this happens, there is a risk that the outward appearance of integration is an illusion. In reality, the cracks between services can be just as deep – and, in some senses, more of a threat because there is now even more to conceal them. (pages 12–13)

A recent report by the NCSL (2006b) has defined two key drivers for multi-agency working, as discussed below.

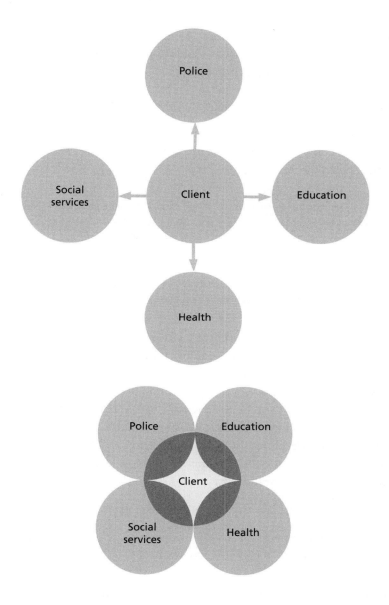

Figure 7.1 From silos to services

Promoting the interests of children

This is particularly well modelled by special schools where there has been a requirement to develop effective provision related directly to the needs of the child. The 1989 Children Act introduced a broader requirement for agencies to collaborate in the interest of vulnerable children. More recently, drives towards the greater personalization of learning have engaged schools in more extended partnerships as the extent of individual needs becomes clearer.

Promoting joined-up thinking

Social exclusion is a multi-faceted problem. If it is to be addressed effectively the solution has to be connected and joined up. Tony Blair, at the launch of the Social Exclusion Unit, stated the challenge:

> Everyone knows that the problems of social exclusion – of failure at school, joblessness, crime – are woven together when you get down to the level of individuals' daily life, of the life on a housing estate. Yet all too often governments in the past have tried to slice problems up into separate packages … And in many areas dozens of agencies and professionals are working in parallel, often doing good things, but sometimes working at cross purposes with far too little coordination and cooperation. Joined up problems, demand joined up solutions. (Social Exclusion Unit, cited in Coleman, 2006, page 9)

The ambitious scale of reform, the changing role of schools and the complex needs of children and families mean that no one organization can achieve its aims alone. Organizational aims are becoming interdependent and collective. One of the drivers of multi-agency working is therefore that this co-ordinated approach is able to deliver results that represent more than simply the sum of the parts. To this end, the term 'collaborative advantage' is now in use and denotes the added value that collaboration can bring. This has been explored in the work of Paton and Vangen (2004), who are clear that collaborations are by nature inefficient and must be used sparingly. They urge those contemplating collaboration to use them only for situations when real collaborative advantage can be envisaged:

> To gain real advantage from any collaboration, something has to be achieved that could not have been achieved by any one of the agencies acting alone. (page 2)

The unselective nature of partnership has also been highlighted as one of the dangers in the current climate by Alexander and Macdonald (2005), which can lead to partnerships failing, additional stress in the system and staff turnover increasing:

> There is a danger in the current climate that everyone is committed to work in multiagency partnership groups, even when this level of formalisation of routine inter-agency communication is not necessary. (page 6)

Collaboration and multi-agency partnerships provide organizations with opportunities to learn. But how good are we at learning from others? In order to be receptive to learning, schools need to shift from a dominator paradigm to one characterized by partnership, say Alfonso Montuori and Isabella Conti (1993). One of the features of moving to partnership is the role of expanded attention:

> Partnership gently directs our attention to an entirely different world, to a universe next door. (page 260)

And in addition:

> We are reminded that partnership is not a struggle between the good guys and the bad guys; that means we can be relieved of self righteousness, and this is an enormous gift, because we can shed the feeling that we have to have all the answers. The need to possess an absolute truth is the legacy of the old paradigm. (page 264)

Schools also need to shift their perspective to one where all resources are equally owned. Teachers are passionate about their own classroom, but this can sometimes spill over into being 'territorial'. This is exemplified in those teachers who, at the end of the day, leave instructions on the whiteboard 'needed for tomorrow, please do not remove', leaving the evening adult education teacher with a key resource that is unavailable. Schools must develop an internal culture which understands that all resources are collectively owned. At the same time, the expectation needs to be built that resources on the school site are to be respected by all who use them:

> The key thing is that people understand that the school is corporately owned. Then the next thing is that people who come in to use the territory understand what the philosophy and rules are about the use of resources. We invite staff from other agencies to our staff meetings so we can all be clear about the expectations. (NCSL, 2006b, page 31)

But it does not come easily to schools:

> The challenge as a head is to broaden your perspective and accept that you now need to work with other agencies, though it is not what you are accustomed to. (page 11)

But a gentle shifting of perspective is becoming apparent:

> I've changed the way I see things through working with others. I'm much less dogmatic now. (page 30)

In practice this can mean:

> We benefit from having the experience of working with people from other backgrounds. We pick up other perspectives and others' ways of doing things. We have skill sharing workshops. All of this enhances the CVs of those involved and enables staff to give real life examples. We can also share resources for training. (Coleman, cited in NCSL, 2006b, page 14)

Power (2004) agrees that opening up professional and organizational expertise to external challenge, scrutiny and questioning can be experienced either as an opportunity or a threat. Individual professions have been built up in ignorance of each other and it is sometimes too easy to be driven back into boxes, and refuse to be exposed to different mindsets and professional practice, particularly in a culture where the public sector is relentlessly called to account and can respond by becoming 'risk averse'.

This notion of schools and other agencies extending their opportunities for organizational learning has been explored by Craig and Perri 6 (2004). They describe schools as needing to shift from a position where, although they are trusted and respected, they have an enduring legacy of authority and this leads to their conducting monologues. This means that schools will need to rethink their manner of engaging in external relationships if they are going to have any legitimacy at all in this multi-sector context. The stakes, as Craig and Perri 6 point out, are indeed enormous, but the prize for children, families and communities is huge:

> The most ambitious extended schools make learning an open book, learning alongside parents, partner agencies and students, welcoming and encouraging leadership from diverse sources. (page 3)

To succeed, extended schools must not only forge new structures but also new cultures. They must root their work in the needs of their students and their community, and learn to exist within open systems of children's services, working to a common purpose.

Delegates at the Better Together series found that an examination of organizational priorities was a useful starting point for establishing a common purpose in partnerships and a better understanding of each sector's core values and mission purpose. Individuals were asked to position themselves at the place on the triangle (Figure 7.2) that most accurately represented the relative emphasis given to three core priorities in their sector. At the Better Together series, these priorities were defined as well-being, standards/achievements and social justice. Only in an extreme case did a delegate position themselves at one of the far corners of the triangle, and they all expressed a wish to be moving to the centre in order to be working on all three priorities interdependently. The exercise stimulated debate on the issues raised in Chapters 1–3; the impact of social justice and well-being on achievement, and the way in which raising standards of achievement and approaches to learning can impact on the enhanced well-being, economic prosperity and social justice in an area. When done in a cross-sector group, the relative position of different agencies becomes apparent but so do the potential points of connection.

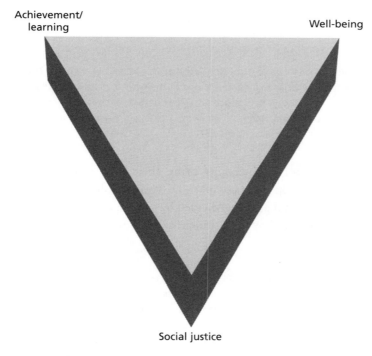

Figure 7.2 The purposes of education

Because we were all standing in the triangle and we could all see each other we had a real sense of community. The triangle was the whole agenda and we all had different things to contribute to it from our own organisational perspective and professional background. This made me as a teacher less concerned, I could see who was fighting for social justice and well being and could see how my work on supporting learning could help them. (delegate on Better Together, 2004)

This helps organizations to find the 'win–win' which is so important in multi-agency partnerships. No one organization can dictate these terms. Craig et al. (2005) have noted that establishing the win–win is an important stage in promoting joint ownership of issues across the partnership. As NCSL (2006a) points out, when a win–win stance is taken, the basis for the initial contact between agencies moves away from 'Can you help me?' to 'How can we help you?', or 'How can we help each other achieve our collective aims?'

The need for clear, shared values that are translated into real changes in structures and practice is reinforced by Lownsbrough and O'Leary (2005):

> The sense of a bigger picture, and of the importance of a shared set of objectives, will become ever-more pertinent as the implications of the schools white paper takes hold. With local authorities moving towards commissioning roles, and extended schools commissioning after-hours provision, leaders will need to learn to give up some power if they are to coordinate a range of different services successfully. (page 38)

> Leaders also stressed the need to make it clear that they are serious about the changes they are making in their organisations. This is one of the ways that structural change can be helpful: rather than seeing new structures as instruments of change themselves, leaders used the process of restructuring to highlight a problem – and send a message of the changes needed in a local area. (page 39)

While all cross-sector partnerships bring their own challenges, schools/health partnerships seem to be the most complex. Dr Philip Graham (2000) has studied this relationship and describes it as being 'divided by an iron curtain of bureaucracy'. These two worlds are characterized by both similarities and differences.

> In both worlds the professionals involved all want the best for children and work hard to achieve it. Both pay lip service to the need to work with parents, and both have great difficulty in working out how to do this, especially with parents they regard as 'over-anxious'. But there are important differences too. Doctors and nurses talk a different language from teachers and interpreters are sometimes necessary. They take quite different attitudes to mental health difficulties, which form the most problematic part of their work with children. (page 1)

His assessment of the similarities and differences provides us with a useful insight into these two worlds.

Similarities

- Both want the best for children and their families.
- Professionals in both are not given the same respect they were.
- Both talk a lot about the whole child but act on 'bits' of children.
- Both often feel 'at sea' when it comes to behavioural difficulties.
- Both are under increasing budgetary and bureaucratic pressure.

Differences

- Relief of symptoms versus developing understanding and learning.
- The language of symptoms versus the language of problems, difficulties and remediation.
- Focus on the individual versus focus on the group.
- Senior doctors continue clinical work versus senior teachers don't.
- Feel underpaid versus really are underpaid.

What makes multi-agency partnerships successful?

There is a significant amount of evidence on what makes multi-agency partnerships successful. NCSL has studied these and drawn up a summary of success factors. These range from factors at a strategic, operational, community and voluntary sector involvement and evaluation-related level.

Strategic

Genuine commitment to joint working.

Effective strategic leadership.

Democracy and equality between groups.

Shared goals and common targets.

Appropriate time frames.

Effective governance.

Sufficient base-line and monitoring data.

Processes for regularly reviewing and monitoring strategic drivers.

Operational

Strong operational leadership.

Clarity of vision and purpose.

Clearly defined roles.

Effective management of human resource issues – pay/joint training/terms and conditions.

Active development of skills needed for multi-agency working.

Building on existing good relationships.

Supporting structures – service-level agreements/management boards and so on.

Good communication and information exchange.

Appropriate referral across agencies.

Agreed risk management systems.

Agreed and coherent exit strategies.

Mechanisms for dealing with conflict and disagreement.

Community and voluntary sector involvement

Mechanisms for engagement and involvement.

Mechanisms for consultation and feedback.

Gaining and demonstrating legitimacy.

Evaluation

Ongoing evaluation of the partnership.

Mechanism for introducing change, which is sufficiently challenging to support future developments. (NCSL, 2006b, page 24)

Multi-agency teams bring the above factors to life as they report on their development as a team. A local authority working with NCSL on the development of its multi-agency team was asked to describe the features of the team when they were working at their best:

- Empower everyone to think differently.
- Create a culture of honesty and understanding.
- Build clarity on the bigger vision so that everyone can own it.
- Review the team's performance at a task level – 'What are we doing?' – and at a process level – 'How are we doing it?'.
- Practise reflective practice and build the time in to do it well.
- Keep focusing on outcomes for children and collectively celebrate every success.

The most critical element in establishing and developing multi-agency partnerships is the development of trust. Establishing this usually requires confronting some well-established conceptions of what it means to be a member of a professional group. Different professions hold myths about each other. These myths will persist as long as professionals have little exposure to alternative professional cultures. A recent NCSL multi-agency team development programme engaged these professionals in a hot-seating activity. A headteacher was asked, 'Why do you treat all children as if they were the same, in batches of 30?' A social worker was asked, 'Why are your standards so low and why can I never get hold of you on the telephone?' Although these questions hurt and challenged the group, working through them collectively allowed the 'myths' to be exposed and the reality of each others' professional lives to creep in to the discourse. This allowed relationships to build across the partnership:

At the end of the day you can put all the structures in, but if the relationships aren't there they don't mean a thing. It's how it's done on a one-to-one basis that is absolutely paramount. (Coleman, cited in NCSL, 2006b, page 26)

Building trust and relationships also means talking about the different language we use and taking the time to understand our own meaning and the meaning of others:

What schools call a code of conduct or a set of rules, youth workers would run a mile from. But they always have ground rules. So long as you can say the code of conduct, is, in a way an agreed set of ground rules which parent voice and pupil voice have already been heavily involved in, they'll say 'ah, lovely, OK we can work with that'. Similarly if you use the term 'confidentiality' across different groups of teachers, health workers, youth workers, and social services, it means hugely different things. (page 27)

The development of ground rules has been found to be particularly beneficial, particularly when some of the partners in the collaboration feel vulnerable or uneasy. Work done by the NCSL has found that posting ground rules in a visible location, modelling the desired behaviour and challenging any early breach of these rules early on are important strategies (NCSL, 2006a).

An example of ground rules that are simple, easy to use and direct are those that are used by the Mental Health Foundation Conference Centre. Ground rules such as these would be familiar to schools and agencies that are building healthy partnerships and using them to aid that process, and are listed below.

Please

Listen to what other people are saying.

Respect the views of others, even if you disagree with them.

Tell us what you think – all views are equally valuable.

Use plain English.

Keep your contribution to the point.

Be positive and concentrate on what can be done, rather than what can't.

Please do not

Feel you have to say something.

Breach others' confidences.

Criticize individuals, organizations or seek to disparage them.

Use abusive or offensive language.

Concentrate on past failures.

(Adapted from Mental Health Foundation Conference Centre, 2006)

Some schools have developed trust among agencies by having a well thought-out induction process for agency staff who work on the school site. This can include provision such as:

- Spending one-to-one time with members of the senior leadership team to get a feel for the school.
- Shadowing a teacher for a day.
- Meeting colleagues from other agencies working in the school and shadowing other key professionals for a day.
- Meeting members of the community over coffee in or outside the school to understand their needs and their role in the school.
- Spending time with colleagues from their own agencies to discuss issues and experiences.

> It can be very daunting for someone who is not a teacher to come into a school – very daunting, almost frightening. But in our staff room we have a policeman, a fireman, a youth worker, learning mentors, a learning support assistant, an attendance officer, an ex-social worker, and health professional. The staff are used to, and welcoming of other agencies. It is a staff room, not a teaching staff room. (Coleman, cited in NCSL, 2006b, page 33)

One of the best examples of cross-sector collaboration is the work done in the Early Years sector and, in particular, the work of Sure Start local programmes. The five early reports from the National Evaluation of Sure Start (NESS) show that Sure Start is succeeding in making a difference to a large number of parents and children, and is doing particularly well in affecting parenting practices and promoting multi-agency working. However, it is still not reaching some of the most disadvantaged families and there is variability of quality across the country.

Sure Start has provided a model of working that engages parents, links local people more directly to the services they require and has implemented a collaborative approach to planning and development. The advice from local Sure Start programme managers, about what works well when working in this way, reinforces other studies of effective multi-agency practice:

- Establish an environment that supports risk and avoids blame.
- Be flexible to meet the real needs of the people the services are intended to help.
- Take steps to promote a genuinely shared vision among partners.
- Remain focused on core business.
- Understand how change affects people.
- Think about sustainability for services from the start and introduce changes, however small, from day one will help to avoid the development of the culture of dependency.

- Build on what you do well.
- Identify shared targets and areas of mutual interest to promote partnership.

Interestingly, where Sure Start has been criticized, it is because it has taken time to get work off the ground, and has been slow in achieving its targets. Those working in the field would say that this is because investing time in building trust, involving service users and building a genuine shared vision, does take time, but leads to sustainable change in people and localities.

The work of Huxham and Vangen (2004) has explored the issues of power and authority in the development of collaborative partnerships. They explored where power lies in partnerships and how this affects the work they are able to do. They see a spectrum of power operating which moves towards greater collaboration and the equitable distribution of power and control.

> From:
> Power over – own gain
> Maintenance of control
> To:
> Power to – mutual gain, means to an end
> Keeps the relationship stable and focused on individual organizational outcomes
> To:
> Power for – altruistic gain for others
> Focuses on moral purpose and collective outcomes
> Empowers others to take on an active role as part of the commitment to long term, sustainable outcomes, (Huxham and Vangen, 2004).

Sure Start has modelled a shift towards 'power for', and has created a multi-sector working environment where the users are empowered to make decisions and take on a leadership role. There is evidence that this model has also started to influence the work of schools.

Stuart McLaughlin, at Falmer High School in Brighton, has set up a multi-agency advice centre for young people that operates after school hours and throughout the holidays. He understands the importance of supporting such a venture but keeping a definite distance from it:

> It's called Mac's place and students can go there for advice on virtually any issue. I make a point of never going there myself; if you're a 16 year old who has come to inquire about emergency contraception the last person you want to bump into is your headteacher. It is incredibly successful and half the students made use of it last year. The young people have their own management group who set rules. (NCSL, 2006b, page 27)

Shotton Hall School, Peterlee, County Durham, has built an advice centre for its students. The centre was designed by the students and is managed by them. They chose the location and made sure it had the right feel and privacy they wanted. Craig (Craig and Perri 6, 2004) reports that:

> If it had been a teacher initiated thing and controlled by adults, it wouldn't have been as well used as it is. This is all about freeing up the dependency culture in this district and showing people they can do things for themselves, rather than having it done for them or to them. (page 17)

A new professionalism?

At the moment, the system is attempting to reconfigure itself into multi-professional teams and is drawing in discrete professionals. To aid this, a common set of skills and areas of knowledge for those working with children is emerging across the system (HM Government, 2005). This aims to develop professionals who are able to promote equality, respect diversity, challenge stereotypes, help to improve the life chances of all children and young people, and provide more effective and integrated services. This common core of knowledge and skills includes:

Communication and team work skills

Assertiveness

Knowledge of others' roles and remit

Understanding the value you bring to the team as an individual

The skills and expertise needed to minimise the need for specialist referral

General knowledge of different organisations and individuals working with children

Knowledge of relevant procedures and working methods

Knowledge of relevant law, policies and procedures.

(HM Government, 2005, pages 18–19)

There is growing interest in a profession that exists across much of Europe but which has no counterpart in the UK at the moment, that of 'social pedagogue'. The social pedagogue has an integrating influence on a range of professional groups, and works in a way that is educative, caring and therapeutic. Social pedagogues operate as agents of society, and work with groups and communities as well as individuals. Davies Jones (2000) sees this European phenomena becoming increasingly relevant to a UK context for a range of reasons: the crisis in residential child care and looked-after children, the extension of Early Years provision, the need for a more coherent approach to youth provision to prevent alienation from society and the need for greater co-operation between the caring and the helping professions. He stresses the need for 'integrating influences' and sees social pedagogues as fulfilling such a role.

Moving from silos to services is a struggle, and it will take time. It takes individuals out of their comfort zone, but opens them up to new learning. It challenges organizations and sectors, particularly those that have enjoyed a somewhat protected and insular existence. Partnerships work best and have the resilience to handle the tough times if the end-user is kept in mind and achieving the best for them overrides all other aims. For example, The Winsford Networked Learning community has been working in a cross-town collaborative for some time now and knows that it's time to 'cut the crap'. They say:

> Local people don't care about who's delivering – just about good services. Territoriality is over with. (Godfrey, 2005, page 16)

Territoriality is definitely over with. As silos move to become joined-up services, those who most need to benefit will do so, if we have the courage to address culture and emotional change as much as the structural change that is currently predominant.

This, in turn, implies a rethinking of the nature of leadership in the community in general, and in the provision of children and young people's services in particular. There are very real issues in moving from silos to services; professional and personal autonomy is one of the most jealously guarded aspects of working life. There are genuine concerns about roles, careers, organizational structures, rights and responsibilities, accountability and compliance:

> But the deeper challenge remains the one with which we began: that of establishing a shared direction across increasingly complex systems and communities, which is rooted in an ethical commitment to all children but is capable of challenging and transcending the specific practices and structures currently used by different groups of professionals.
>
> The everyday practice of leadership is central to meeting this challenge, precisely because leadership enables people to take risks and go beyond their familiar practice. In every authority, and probably in every neighbourhood, this shared imperative is likely to create specific opportunities for development – shared learning opportunities across separate organisations, informal networks which involve parent and families in new ways, common approaches to professional learning and workforce development. (Lownsbrough and O'Leary, 2005, pages 83–84)

Part 3

Building capacity in communities

8 Leadership in the community

Introduction

Leadership is fundamental to every change and initiative discussed in Part 2 of this book. But just as the various strategies described involve a fundamental reconceptualization of the nature, role and purpose of the school, so there is a parallel need to rethink the nature of leadership. In many ways the shift from bonding to bridging described in Chapter 2 epitomizes the scope and scale of the change required. This chapter develops a model of leadership to meet the needs of the new situation by reviewing:

- The characteristics of effective leadership
- The nature of leadership beyond the school
- The movement towards shared leadership
- Leadership qualities and behaviours
- Developing leadership
- The National Standards for Headteachers.

The characteristics of effective leadership

Leadership is an elusive and contested concept, the subject of profound academic debate and widely varying popular usage. Yet there does seem to be a deep-seated consensus that effective leadership is essential to the success of any organization, project or social activity. It is possible to demonstrate a very high correlation between the quality of leadership and the success of a school, sports team, military unit, political party or any community. Indeed poor or inappropriate leadership will be one of the explanations (and scapegoats) of failure in any social venture. Team captains resign, generals are promoted and chief executives are sacked as the first response to any social unit failing to achieve its stated purpose. While this may often be unfair, it does demonstrate the extent to which our cultural expectations focus on a leader or the leadership of the organization, and most models of accountability reinforce the centrality and significance of leaders and leadership.

This focus on leadership is an implicit recognition of the ultimate importance that we attach to those aspects of organizational life that are most closely associated with the work of leaders. Again, there are numerous interpretations and permutations available but it does seem reasonable to argue that leadership is predominantly concerned with three fundamental components of any form of social activity:

1. Establishing the values by which the organization will function.
2. Defining the core purpose of the organization.
3. Securing the commitment and engagement of people to live the values and achieve the purpose.

Although there is a danger of a *reductio ad absurdum*, the interaction of these three elements seems to encompass most of what is generally accepted and understood about the distinctive nature of leadership. In *Good to Great*, Collins (2001) identifies the five levels of engagement in organizational life; level 5 is essentially the culmination of the previous four levels:

LEVEL 5 EXECUTIVE

Builds enduring greatness through a paradoxical blend of personal humility and professional will.

LEVEL 4 EFFECTIVE LEADERSHIP

Catalyzes commitment to and vigorous pursuit of a clear and compelling vision, stimulating higher performance standards.

LEVEL 3 COMPETENT MANAGER

Organizes people and recourses towards the effective and efficient pursuit of pre-determined objectives.

LEVEL 2 CONTRIBUTING TEAM MEMBER

Contributes individual capabilities to the achievement of group objectives and works effectively with others in a group setting.

LEVEL 1 HIGHLY CAPABLE INDIVIDUAL

Makes productive contributions through talent, knowledge, skills and good work habits.
(page 20)

Sergiovanni (2001) points to the need to move away from the 'leader as hero' and the 'leader as bureaucrat' to a different model altogether:

> What kind of leadership will be needed for schools to effectively serve society as we look further into the future? Whatever the answer, it will not be the superhero leadership of the past. The new century will not be kind to leaders who seek to change things by sheer force of their personality. Nor will it be kind to leaders who seek to change things by the sheer force of their bureaucratic authority. Instead, we will need leadership for schools themed to learning, to the development of civic virtue, and to the cultivation of self-management.
> (page 38)

Seeing leadership as concerned with values, purpose and people is, of course, content and context free. It could be applied to a criminal gang as much as to a school or community. This is where the debate in Part 1 of this book becomes important – for our purposes in this discussion, the core values of leadership are social justice, equity, inclusion and access to educational opportunities for all. The purpose of leadership in education is to develop policies and strategies to secure the values, and the focus on people is both to ensure their commitment and to model the principles in practice.

Underpinning all three elements, and elemental to any definition of leadership based on change, is the fundamental precept that leadership is about change, innovation and creativity. If we lived in an ideal world where all our aspirations had been met then it would only be necessary to manage the status quo. As it is, achieving social justice, for virtually every society in the world, implies change – and that is why leadership is so vitally important.

The nature of leadership beyond the school

All of the principles outlined above have been known and understood for many years; sadly they have not always been applied. Where they have been applied it has almost always been to the school as an institution. Educational leadership has been seen as synonymous with school leadership. Part 2 of this book has argued for a new perspective in which leadership in education encompasses a broader perspective. This change can be best summarized as moving from 'bonding', in other words leadership focused on the integrity of the school, to 'bridging', or the school engaging with the wider community. The implications of this change are summarized in Figure 8.1.

From	To
Focus on the school	Focus on the community
Accountability for academic attainment	Accountability for educational outcomes
Leadership of professional staff	Leadership across the community
Leadership limited by time and place	No boundaries of time and place
Working in professional silos	Working across agencies
Leadership as hierarchy	Leadership widely distributed
Leadership related to professional status	Leadership related to need and context
Institutional improvement	Community development
Bonding	Bridging

Figure 8.1 The changing nature of educational leadership

Hargreaves and Fink (2006) capture the essence of this change:

> The hardest part of sustainable leadership is the part that provokes us to think beyond our own schools and ourselves. It is the part that calls us to serve the public good of all people's children within and beyond our community and not only the private interests of those who subscribe to our own institution. Sustainable leadership means caring for all the people our actions and choices affect – those whom we can't immediately see as well as those whom we can. (page 158)

Leadership beyond the school has significant implications for those who hold traditional leadership roles – in essence, the boundaries of their roles will be extended – they will have to work with increasingly wide horizons.

Table 8.1 offers a possible typology of systems leadership. However, it would be a mistake to imagine that this is a recent phenomenon, although it has been highly variable (and therein lies the problem); headteachers have always had responsibility for, and engagement with, matters over and above the integrity of their own school. However, this was often on an 'opting-in' or representative basis. The primary focus, professional expectation and models of accountability saw leadership of the individual school as the key defining characteristic of headship. By a range of criteria, that focus is now changing.

Table 8.1 A typology of systems leadership

7	Advising on national policies and strategies	Direct involvement with DfES through associations, think tanks, advisory bodies
6	Collaborating with other agencies	Working in the context of the Children Act
5	Working for local authorities	Advisory work, consultant leaders, school improvement partners, guidance on policy
4	Leading community initiatives	Active partnership and involvement across community initiatives
3	Leading networks, clusters and federations	Varying degrees of responsibility and authority over the work of other schools
2	Executive leadership	Direct involvement in the leadership of a second or third school
1	Leadership of extended schools	Changing responsibility in terms of time, resources, space and activity

The typology in Table 8.1 could be seen as a series of concentric circles or waves moving from a central point – leadership – in education, through a series of stages each one further removed from the traditional model of headship. Another way to picture this would be as a vector with each stage representing a further step away from the school, raising the possibility of professional leadership in education that is not school based (as shown in Figure 8.2).

School leadership

Figure 8.2 The scope of systems leadership

The movement through the stages from level 1 to level 7 is characterized by a number of factors:

- Fewer opportunities for direct control.
- Greater emphasis on negotiation and influence.
- Increasingly vague accountability.
- Increasing uncertainty and ambiguity.
- Greater potential to inform system change.
- Less direct involvement with school.
- Working in the context of more diffuse outcomes.
- Diminishing confidence about impact.

These changes might be best represented by the model shown in Figure 8.3.

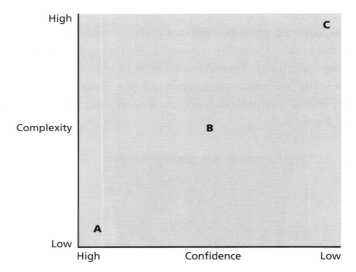

Figure 8.3 Leading beyond the school

The work of an experienced and successful headteacher might be characterized as high confidence and low complexity (point A); the components of successful school leadership are well known and understood, and there are few situations that represent a significant professional challenge. However, the movement to point B and beyond may well represent an increase in the complexity of the activities undertaken and a consequent reduction in confidence unless appropriate development strategies are in place. In essence, as in all learning and development, point A is always moving and effective leaders need to be able to recognize the ever-changing relationship between complexity and confidence.

It may be helpful to see this as a journey with an ever-receding horizon. The sea-trade routes of antiquity tended to follow the coastline – to aid navigation and provide shelter from storms and pirates. It was an act of considerable courage to move out of sight of land, away from the certainties of known landmarks, routines and procedures. It is sometimes argued that the move from deputy to headteacher is one of the most significant changes in role – the move from headteacher to system leader may be of a greater order of magnitude given the changing scope of the work involved, as identified above.

Bryk and Schneider (2002) highlight the imperatives and problems in moving beyond the school:

> Thus it becomes incumbent on teachers to acknowledge these parental vulnerabilities and actively reach out to moderate them. Unfortunately, such responsibilities often are not acknowledged as a critical aspect of teachers' roles and may be addressed unevenly, if at all, in many schools. … Strengthening the social base for engaging students, teachers, and parents around more ambitious learning, however, also is essential. (page 138)

> … elementary school teachers spend the vast majority of their time engaged with children. Little in their professional socialization or formal training prepares them for working with parents and other adults in the community. (page 139)

> Thus, our research suggest that effective urban schools need teachers that not only know their students well, but also have an empathetic understanding of their parents' situations and have the interpersonal skills needed to engage these adults effectively. (page 139)

However, it would be wrong to underestimate the potential impact and implications of this change. The mental landscape of most school leaders is, properly and understandably, focused on the leadership of an institution – and schools are still very much creations of the nineteenth century.

The movement to the school as a community within communities requires an acceptance of the abandonment of what Zohar (1997, page 53) defines as the old paradigm and the acceptance of a new paradigm (Table 8.2).

Table 8.2 Acceptance of abandonment paradigms

Old paradigm		New paradigm
Reductive	versus	Emergent
Isolated and controlled	versus	Contextual and self-organizing
The parts completely define the whole	versus	The whole is greater than the sum of its parts
Top-down management	versus	Bottom-up leadership
Reactive	versus	Imaginative and experimental

Hock (1999) extends this concept of a new paradigm in what he defines as a chaordic organization:

> Chaord ...
>
> 1. any self-organizing, self-governing, adaptive, nonlinear, complex organism, organization, community or system, whether physical, biological or social, the behavior of which harmoniously blends characteristics of both chaos and order. 2. an entity whose behavior exhibits observable patterns and probabilities not governed or explained by the rules that govern or explain its constituent parts. (frontispiece)

He details the implications for leadership of working in chaordic organizations in chaordic communities in a chaordic world:

> Just as we are citizens of a city, province, or nation by right of birth, so too are we citizens of the world, for we were most certainly born there also. We are no less citizens of corporations, churches, and countless other organizations by right of choice. If we do not develop new and better concepts of organization and leadership wherein persuasion prevails over power, reason over emotion, trust over suspicion, hope over fear, cooperation over coercion and liberty over tyranny, we shall never harness science or technology in the service of humanity, let alone in the service of all other creatures and the living earth on which we depend. (page 209)

What Zohar, Hock and countless others point to is what we all intuitively know. The prescribed curriculum, scheme of work, lesson plan and timetable bear no real relationship to the reality of learning in the classroom. The holiday never coincides precisely with the itinerary; the battle is never fought as planned by the generals; life at 60 is rarely what we envisaged at 20.

The movement towards shared leadership

Just as the role of individual leaders will change, so will our conceptualization of who leaders are. In essence, the movement is from a focus on the status of the leader to seeing leadership as a collective capacity, in other words as a resource available from multiple sources. The change can be represented diagrammatically, as in Figure 8.4.

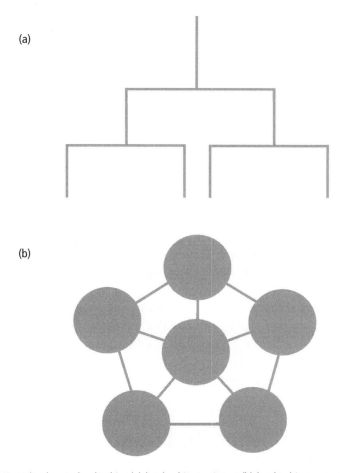

(a)

(b)

Figure 8.4 From leaders to leadership: (a) leadership as status; (b) leadership as capacity

In the traditional model, leadership is related to relative status in the organization – there will be a defined level at which individuals move from being a 'non-leader' to being a leader. This can actually be reflected in career structures and formal definitions of salary scales – as though promotion confers leadership qualities and capabilities.

Shared leadership does not preclude the existence of leaders – rather it changes their role and status. Shared leadership implies an approach to leadership that is functional

– who leads is determined by context, need and appropriateness. Thus, the criteria for who leads are based on knowledge, aptitude, skills, networks and credibility. Status is no guarantee of capability. The movement towards shared leadership implies a number of significant conceptual shifts:

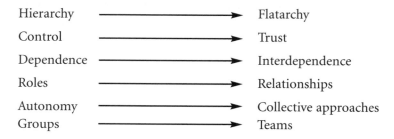

Hierarchy	⟶ Flatarchy
Control	⟶ Trust
Dependence	⟶ Interdependence
Roles	⟶ Relationships
Autonomy	⟶ Collective approaches
Groups	⟶ Teams

Many headteachers in England are happy when their school's governing body includes somebody with expertise in finance or personnel issues. Very often these people will provide leadership in their area of specialization. Shared leadership is an extension of this principle of leadership based on expertise.

The movement from the hierarchal structure, shown in Figure 8.4, to a more open, possibly team-based approach, enables the possibility of leadership being shared across the school and the community. It implies teachers being actively engaged in leading community projects, students having genuine authority, parents being involved in authentic decision making and the whole community having a sense of investment in learning.

In a society that in many ways remains deferential, and where queuing is a national pastime, it would be wrong to underestimate the challenge of shared leadership. It requires a simultaneous willingness to surrender authority and to accept it. It means that leaders have to be comfortable with following and followers will have to accept responsibility, authority and accountability.

Leadership qualities and behaviours

Putnam's (2003, page 294) powerful image of 'reweaving social webs' points to a very particular type of leadership; he refers to 'local leaders', not those imported by virtue of qualifications or experience but rather anyone who has the potential to contribute to the development of the community. This immediately raises serious issues about the personal qualities of such leaders as they will often lack the 'power derived from position' that is the source of leadership authority for many. Conventional views of leadership qualities and behaviours may not be appropriate in the context of community leadership given:

- the lack of organizational status;
- the complexity of relationships;
- the multiple perspectives operating;
- the absence of formal, contractual relationships;
- the lack of a management infrastructure.

In essence, people cannot be forced to collaborate and network, and there are not the usual sanctions associated with organizational life.

Leadership therefore has to work in very different ways in the context of community development and it seems appropriate that the characteristics of leaders should be derived from the context in which they are working, in other words that 'form' should follow 'function' in the well-known design adage. Whatever the context – classroom, team, school, community-based project, liaison between agencies – it can be argued that the 'function' of leadership is to create communities of different types. It might be appropriate, therefore, to see this 'form' of leadership as creating and sustaining communities, in other words building social capital. The qualities and behaviours of leadership might best be described in terms of building and sustaining social capital, as outlined in Chapter 2.

Quintessentially, the most appropriate leadership behaviours are those that create social capital through bonding and bridging. It is therefore possible to relate leadership characteristics and behaviours to the components of social capital:

- Shared social norms and values: leaders actively articulate norms and values; initiate rich conversations and dialogue about them; reinforce and celebrate appropriate behaviour; and challenge inappropriate behaviour. Crucially, they secure alignment, informed consensus and recognize that beliefs and values are emergent – always developing.

- Sophisticated social networks: leaders enable and sustain rich and sophisticated networks through facilitation, making connections and empowering individuals. Leaders facilitate dialogue (see Chapter 10) and help create a common language.

- High levels of trust: leaders share power and authority through empowerment; they build leadership capacity in others by recognizing and reinforcing potential. In Bryk and Schneider's (2002) terms they do this through 'respect, competence, personal regard for others and integrity' (page 23).

- High civic engagement: leaders secure involvement and participation in the community through their personal credibility, understanding the motivation of community members and ensuring that decision-making processes are real, significant and make an impact.

- Symbols and rituals: leaders are aware that people need to be able to publicly recognize and celebrate their membership of a community. Leaders foster a sense of unity, pride and commitment, and publicly endorse the community.

- Interdependence and reciprocity: leaders model high-quality interpersonal relationships, positive mutual regard and are acutely sensitive to their emotional impact on others. Crucially, leaders exemplify a sophisticated level of 'caring and sharing'.
- Volunteering and community action: leaders demonstrate in their own behaviour that successful communities do not 'work to rule'. Leaders join in, are not status conscious, and initiate and support collaborative action.
- Above all, leaders need to act.

In his study of why societies succeed or collapse, Diamond (2005) summarizes the necessary approach:

> Of course, though, people with long-term stakes don't always act wisely. Often they still prefer short-term goals, and often again they do things that are foolish in both the short term and the long term. That's what makes biography and history infinitely more complicated and less predictable than the courses of reactions ... Leaders who don't just react passively, who have the courage to anticipate crises or to act early, and who make strong insightful decisions of top-down management really can make a huge difference to their societies. So can similarly courageous, active citizens practising bottom-up management. (page 306)

This is a highly intimidating list, a 'council of perfection', and it provides another challenge to leadership orthodoxy – it may well be that such a combination of virtues will not be found in one person – it will need shared leadership to ensure all of these characteristics are in place. Equally, these characteristics are only rarely fully formed in any person – they have to be learned, developed and nourished.

Developing leadership

The approach to leadership that has been described in this chapter is not going to be developed by sending people on courses or by reading books. Leaders tend to go on leadership courses, which are very often high-status events that tend to confirm rather than challenge. Only in recent years have we seen a movement towards leadership programmes that are open to all and are concerned with preparing for leadership. The steady movement towards shared leadership in schools, the slowly emerging concept of teacher leadership in the classroom and the increasing recognition of leadership development for students are all hopeful signs. However, it is still rare for school support staff (the very term is worrying) to be offered leadership development and rarer still for schools to share leadership development with their wider communities, notably governors and parents. It is still unusual for leadership development to be shared across all the agencies concerned with children and young people. This issue is essentially cultural and attitudinal – and may take years to change. What we can be more confident about is our changing understanding of what is needed to ensure that leadership development actually works – whoever is engaged in it.

There is a number of fundamental principles that seem to inform leadership development that actually makes an impact on those who participate:

1. *Leadership development is rooted in learning.*

   This means that leadership development programmes have to be concerned with the learning of the individual rather than the transmission of information to the group. In essence, this involves the creation of personal knowledge and understanding that is focused on beliefs, attitudes and behaviours.

2. *Leadership development involves challenge.*

   We create knowledge and understanding, and the capacity to change; to the extent we are challenged. This is not about intimidation but rather questioning assumptions, habituated practice and fundamental beliefs. Leadership development seems to work best when groups are allowed to review existing practice against alternative models, case studies and theoretical perspectives.

3. *Leadership development requires reflection.*

   Knowledge and understanding are created by the thoughtful response to challenge. Reflection is the vehicle that allows us to make sense of our prior learning in a new context – reflection is about analysis, insight, clarifying, prioritizing and, gradually, developing a new set of beliefs about self and the world.

4. *Leadership development needs support.*

   Effective learning is a social relationship. This can take many forms but perhaps the most potent and effective learning relationship is mentoring and coaching. The one-to-one relationship is fundamental to effective and appropriate challenge, sustained and meaningful reflection and, in the development of appropriate strategies, for action and feedback on their success. Mentoring and coaching actually exemplify many of the leadership behaviours discussed above.

5. *Leadership development is collaborative.*

   In addition to the direct personal support of mentoring and coaching, leadership development is enhanced by rich and sustained interaction with other learners. This can be done through teams in the workplace (indeed, part of the definition of an effective team is that it enables the learning of its members) and the creation of leaning sets.

6. *Leadership development is work based.*

   As has been stressed several times in this chapter, leadership is about action. Leadership is defined and judged to the extent to which it makes a difference: crucially in the way it translates principle into practice. Leadership development is most effective when it is located in people's actual jobs – the best way to learn to lead is by actually leading – with all the principles outlined above in place. Leadership development has to be action learning – learning by doing; being engaged in real and significant tasks but having the support necessary to learn while doing.

In many ways Wenger (1998) captures both the essence of community and the principles of effective learning in his model of communities of practice:

> Students go to school and, as they come together to deal in their own fashion with the agenda of the imposing institution and the unsettling mysteries of youth, communities of practice sprout everywhere – in the classroom as well as on the playground, officially or in the cracks. And in spite of curriculum, discipline, and exhortation, the learning that is most personally transformative turns out to be the learning that involves membership in these communities of practice. (page 6)

> Communities of practice are an integral part of our daily lives. They are so informal and so pervasive that they rarely come into explicit focus, but for the same reasons they are also quite familiar. (page 7)

> Communities of practice are important because their practice:
>
> 1. provides resolutions to institutionally generated conflicts such as contradictions between measures and work – for instance, processing claims versus time on the phone
>
> 2. supports a communal memory that allows individuals to do their work without needing to know everything
>
> 3. helps newcomers join the community by participating in its practice
>
> 4. generates specific perspectives and terms to enable accomplishing what needs to be done
>
> 5. makes the job habitable by creating an atmosphere in which the monotonous and meaningless aspects of the job are woven into the rituals, customs, stories, events, dramas, and rhythms of community life. (page 46)

Leadership development through communities of practice has the potential to:

- build leadership capacity;
- enhance the community;
- build social capital;
- model effective leadership.

The National Standards for Headteachers

In 2004, the DfES in England published revised national standards for headteachers. A major departure from the previous standards and a significant innovation was the inclusion of a standard relating to school leadership and the community.

National Standards for Headteachers (England)

Strengthening community through collaboration

Schools exist in an individual social context, which has a direct impact on what happens inside the school. School leadership should commit to engaging with the internal and external school community, thus modelling the principles of equity and entitlement. Headteachers should encourage and engage in collaboration with other schools in order to bring positive benefits to their own organization and share its expertise more widely. Headteachers should ensure collaboration and collective responsibility for the well-being of children with parents and carers and across multiple agencies, at both strategic and operational levels. Headteachers should be aware that school and community improvement is interdependent and that they share responsibility for leadership of the wider educational system.

Knowledge
Knows about:

- Current issues and future trends that impact on the school community.
- The rich and diverse resources within the local community – both human and physical.
- The wider curriculum beyond school and the opportunities it provides for students and the school community.
- Models of school, home, community and business partnerships.
- The work of other agencies and opportunities for collaboration.
- Strategies that encourage parents to support their children's learning.
- The strengths, capabilities and objectives of other local schools.

Personal qualities
Is committed to:

- Effective team work within the school and with external partners.
- Working with other agencies for the well-being of all pupils and their families.
- Involving parents and the community in supporting the learning of children and indefining and realizing the school vision.
- Networking and collaboration between schools.

Is able to:

- Recognize and take account of the richness and diversity of the school's communities.
- Engage in a dialogue that builds partnerships and community consensus on values, beliefs and shared responsibilities.

- Listen to, reflect and act on community feedback.
- Build and maintain effective relationships with parents, partners and the community that enhance the education for all pupils.

Actions
- Builds a school culture and curriculum which takes account of the richness and diversity of the school's communities.
- Creates and promotes positive strategies for developing good race relations and dealing with racial harassment.
- Ensures learning experiences for pupils are linked into and integrated with the wider community.
- Ensures a range of community-based learning experiences.
- Collaborates with other agencies in providing for the intellectual, spiritual, moral, social and cultural well-being of pupils and their families.
- Creates and maintains an effective partnership with parents to support and improve pupils' achievement and personal development.
- Seeks opportunities to invite local community figures, businesses or organizations into the school to enhance and enrich the curriculum.
- Networks and shares best practice with other schools.

(Adapted from DfES, 2004, page 12)

9 Community action

Introduction

Community participation is now seen as essential to the reform of public services. As services move to become more locally responsive, and the government realizes that centrally prescribed reform will only get us so far in addressing some of the problems outlined in Chapters 1–3, the community has taken centre stage.

Within education, schools have become keen to define their community and indeed to define 'community' per se. This became a preoccupation at one of the Better Together seminars, and actually became a distraction. The very fact that professionals need to define and understand a concept before they can engage with it is part of the problem. Communities are multi-faceted and changing. They can be determined by geographical location, faith, interests, needs, culture or function. They are expressed through a range of symbols which denote community identity: clothing, music, flags, badges, hairstyles and language. They link through spontaneous face-to-face contact, through organized events or through cyberspace. Craig and O'Leary (2005) define community as 'informal networks of shared meaning which hold some intrinsic value for their members'. (page 5)

This chapter will examine:

- The principles of community action
- The role of schools in community action
- Strategies to support community action
- Where next?

The principles of community action

Community action is diffuse, sometimes sporadic, non linear, sometimes unplanned and always enacted through mobilizing people:

> Community workers have long recognised the skills of mobilising people to make a difference that organisations are just now beginning to understand and wrestle with. They are skilled at working across social environments and organisational cultures and are more comfortable in dealing with the more uncertain environment where local action and change is rooted. They are motivated by social justice and mutual respect. (SCCD, 2001, page 5)

Community action lies at the heart of a range of policy areas being pursued today, where the issues are multi-faceted and complex, and the aims challenging:

- building social inclusion;
- building community capacity;
- generating (and spending) social capital;
- promoting personalized approaches to service provision;
- enabling user voice in public-sector reform;
- demanding better services and therefore improving quality.

Because the policy context is so complex, unless the community and the public sector join forces and act together, the public sector in particular is in danger of losing its way.

> Across public policy, from antisocial behaviour to political disengagement, to regeneration – the capacity to engage and lead communities is an increasingly vital limiting factor in our ability to meet shared objectives. (Craig and O'Leary, 2005, page 2)

Community action has a strong values base, through which is enacted:

- Social justice – enabling people to claim their right, speaking out for injustice, having control over decisions that affect them, lobbying for change.
- Participation – moving from consultation to participation.
- Equality – challenging attitudes and practices that marginalize and discriminate.
- Learning – recognizing the skills and knowledge of others and promoting the development of new skills.
- Co-operation and mutualism – working together for mutual benefit.

(Gilchrist, 2004, page 22)

Necessary to any model of community action is the concept of the network. Networks are essential to human interaction and action, and they can take many different forms. In many ways a network is a generic term that covers multiple manifestations, but there does seem to be agreement that an effective network is a powerful resource because:

- 'The whole is greater than the sum of the parts.'
- Networks initiate, build, reinforce and consolidate social relationships.
- Networks can foster innovation and creativity, improve the quality of problem solving and so facilitate change.
- Networks can enhance and maximize the flow of information.

When they work well, networks are fundamental to building social capital through trust, commitment and interdependency. Networks can be small and formal, large and informal, highly centralized or totally distributed. They can be focused on a specific project or generic interests; they can be tightly geographical or, literally, virtual. What is essential to all networks is exchange and sharing. De Geus (1998) illustrates the importance of this process of sharing in the story of milk bottles, blue tits and robins. Both species of birds learned to drink cream from milk bottles when, in the first part of the twentieth century, they were delivered without tops. When aluminium bottle tops were introduced, between the World Wars, the birds lost easy access to their somewhat unorthodox diet, but:

> By the early 1950s, the entire blue tit population of the UK – about a million birds – had learned how to pierce the aluminium seals. Regaining access to this rich food source provided an important victory for the blue tit family as a whole; it gave them an advantage in the battle for survival. Conversely the robins, as a family, never regained access to the cream.
>
> In short, the blue tits went through an extraordinarily successful institutional learning process. The robins failed, even though individual robins had been as innovative as individual blue tits … The explanation … could be found only in the *social propagation* process: the way blue tits spread their skill from one individual to members of the species as a whole.
>
> Birds that flock … seem to learn faster. They increase their chances of surviving and evolving more quickly. (pages 161–162)

The blue tits engaged in community action, the robins were totally unable to do so. Hargreaves (2003) identifies the principles for community action in schools:

- identifying the main areas for transformation and securing collective ownership of them;
- creating a climate of trust among the stakeholders;
- laying down an appropriate infrastructure, both social (networks) and physical (ICT);

- encouraging schools to use this social capital to mobilize their intellectual capital in innovation;
- enhancing the organizational capital of all school leaders;
- respecting the self-organizing systems and spontaneous order within the education service;
- brokering key partnerships to ensure that the process of continuous innovation and knowledge transfer thrives as the hubs change in the light of new themes and priorities for innovation. (page 73)

The spirit of reciprocity, mutualism and empowerment is the engines of community action. Many approaches to address social inequality have started with a premise that is antithetical to this. Many public-sector initiatives assume the community has problems, and the policy and professionals' role is to 'fix it'. For Trevino and Trevino (2004), who have explored the spirit of reciprocity and mutual assistance in California, these approaches are doomed to failure. They describe a mutual assistance approach that deepens the capacity of the communities to act for their own betterment and on their own behalf. They are quick to point out that mutual assistance is not 'business as usual' and it does not happen on its own , but requires a new mindset on everyone's part, particularly if the public sector and professionals are to play a part. The key components of mutual assistance include:

- relying on community residents to initiate projects;
- building the skills of community residents to organize themselves to meet their own needs;
- focusing the desires and potential of community residents to secure a better future;
- actively encouraging families to engage in decision making, governance and goal setting;
- building authentic and reciprocal partnerships between public and private institutions and the community.

The aims of mutual assistance are no different in their intent to those held by the public sector, but the difference is that those involved in mutual assistance know that to achieve them requires new ways of knowing ourselves and others:

- Rekindled hope – reminding communities that 'together we can do anything'.
- Development of leadership – seek out and support natural local leaders.
- Creation of power – unleashing currently unrecognized transformative power in communities.
- Creation of a wisdom bank – collecting and communicating valuable knowly-how.
- Partnering – the promotion of networks within and across communities to ensure sustainability and constant learning and growth.
- Positive long-term relationships – based on trust, reciprocity and communication.
- Maximized resources – using volunteering to leverage resource, and maximum use of seed corn money (the capital investment to support innovation).
- Mutuality – no one expects to receive anything without returning something.

- Community data – the building of real and useful data about which programmes work and which do not.

Most importantly, mutual assistance is not a public service, but a personal and community-based process whereby people come to value their collective impact on a community:

> The one sided nature of current service delivery strips people of their dignity and deprives them of the fundamental and empowering act of returning goods or value. (Trevino and Trevino, 2004, page 3)

The roots of this work can be seen in the work of Paulo Freire, the Brazilian educator and visionary who viewed education as a means of liberation. His work has contributed to a sense of purpose and identity among some of the most dispossessed and marginalized groups in society. He guards against an unjust social order that enables those in power to appear 'generous'. He contrasts this with true generosity:

> False generosity constrains the fearful and subdued, 'the rejects of society' to extend their trembling hands. Real generosity lies in striving so that those hands, whether of individuals or entire communities – need to be extended less and less in supplication and become human hands that work, and by working, transform the world. (Freire, 1972, page 22)

The role of schools in community action

Craig and O'Leary (2005) are clear that schools have an obvious role to play in supporting community action. They believe that schools have the potential to help develop and re-shape relations between citizens and the state, and to engage whole communities in learning in its broadest sense. They also remark that schools have been slow to realize this:

> In a sense the agenda has been slow to arrive for schools. While Health Education Zones and Sure Start focussed heavily on public engagement in New Labour's first term, the legacy of the standards agenda, until very recently, completely superseded the priority of community leadership. (page 7)

The coalition of community schools in the US is also clear that creating and sustaining a community school is a community enterprise (Coalition for Community Schools, 2003). Furthermore, when school reform is aligned with a strong community building and engagement mindset, the school dramatically increases its chance of the reform being sustainable. Community school engagement has been shown to lead to more positive attitudes, expectations and participation among parents, teachers and students. The Texas Alliance brought together 118 schools and community members who signed a declaration to transform the schools into locally responsive and accountable neighbourhood centres. The result was powerful – the schools showed a 42 per cent increase in children passing the state test and attendance rates in the new 'Alliance' schools have risen year on year and are now above average for the state.

In recent years, traditional methods of involving parents and community in schools were seen to have failed in Santa Fe, New Mexico. Schools therefore worked with the Center for RelationaLearning, under a grant from the Charles Stuart Mott Foundation, to design a networking approach to interacting with parents and the community. This approach would be to develop and build social capital as a primary goal of the community involvement strategy. The project centres on 'public conversations' involving common interest groups (for example, all parents or all teachers) who are trained and facilitated in public conversation skills and then moved into mixed interest groups where the trusting relationships between parents, students, teachers and community members that are needed to improve educational provision can be established. Broader networks of communication are established between people who often talk only to people like them. Networking skills are intentionally developed to:

- enhance deliberative and civic skills;
- promote community involvement in education and collaborative problem solving;
- focus on improving teaching and learning;
- generate new understanding of and commitment to education;
- use public conversation as a means to improve education.

By intentionally creating rich and sophisticated networks of relationships where members of the school and community can collectively address pressing educational issues and concerns, parents, students, teachers, administration and community leaders work better together. This networking strategy continues to inform policy, develop social capital, strengthen engagement and release human potential. The Santa Fe schools changed the educational system by teaching networking skills to community members and by developing diverse networks of stakeholders. This system of community involvement is still active and in place six years after its inception.

Networking is designed to transform the current network of relationships as the route to making the system more effective. The project in Santa Fe has the following transformational features. (1) It focuses on educational improvement and reform through the active involvement of all stakeholders. (2) It creates a common skill base to support interaction. (3) It reinforces and enhances engagement with different people and ideas as a preferred way of learning and working together. (4) It creates rich and sophisticated networks of relationships focused on educational change. Following the research in complexity science we believe that our educational system is not just broken but more aptly archaic and inappropriate. Living systems theory suggests that human systems survive, develop and transform by experiencing, owning and integrating differences. Networks and networking provide tools for learning in the community.

In order for schools to take up their role they need to look deeply into their own practice. Leaders in schools need to examine their own intentions and ask 'Whose agenda is being addressed here?'. Schools must reach out to local people and discover who are the natural community leaders. Schools can become sites of community action and engagement by promoting volunteering, internships, licensing of additional learning opportunities, training and development, and paid employment in the community. Schools can also work with the community to invest in 'third spaces' jointly owned and maintained – these third spaces can create an open space where mutually beneficial partnerships may develop.

The extended school day is providing schools with a bridge to link community action with the work of the school:

> We have focused our out of hours work on volunteering and community action. This has opened the doors to a number of organisations and really started to change our relationship with the local community. The youngsters feel they are making a difference to their local area and having fun at the same time. (NCSL, 2005b, page 9)

The Community Pride initiatives in Salford and Manchester have set up 'schools of participation'. The idea comes from Latin America where 'schools' were set up for people to share experiences and learn skills that would enable them to have more control over what was happening in their communities. This is an interesting concept – as it takes a well-established organizational word, 'school', and turns it into something dynamic and different. The schools are primarily aimed at local people aged 16 upwards from grassroots groups and organizations in the voluntary and community sector, they are community led, participative and action oriented. One glance at the key characteristics of the School of Participation is enough to see that they are very different from conventional schools:

- Participants set their own agenda and design their own curriculum. Time, venue and numbers of sessions are all negotiated with participants through a transparent process.
- Participants do not join a school as individuals but come representing a local group or organization and are accountable back to them.
- Numbers of participants can range from eight to 25.
- Schools have 'facilitators' who work as a team, supporting the participants through their learning process.
- Schools offer a mentoring scheme to individual participants.
- Schools offer certification and/or some form of accreditation.

- The school is free, venues are accessible for everyone and help with transport, childcare, interpreters and other support will be provided for participants as necessary.

- An 'exit strategy' is agreed with participants, and any follow-up needs are identified.

- Regular reflections are undertaken to avoid creating a culture of dependency among participants.

- A school results in some form of agreed action for change.

For schools this means overcoming tendencies of 'territoriality' and generating more open access, while at the same time ensuring that when children are in school they are safe. It also means that schools need to begin to have conversations about spaces that are 'neutral', and to explore how they can be mobilized as learning spaces. Schools are beginning to ask questions such as 'Where does the classroom begin and end?', 'Can the community be viewed as an extended classroom?' and 'How can our resources, both financial and human, be used to support community learning spaces for the benefit of all children?'. In other words, schools can foster the growth of 'third spaces' in which they can meet with communities on an equal basis and on neutral territory:

> This means creating social spaces which allow everyday life back into schools and school into everyday life. At the moment schools feel like prisons, not community spaces. (Craig and O'Leary, 2005, page 24)

Spacemakers (www.publicartonline.org.uk) is an organization dedicated to generating new community spaces with the community they will serve. Spacemakers recently completed a two-year project in which young people, aged between 13 and 15, designed a public space within their own community in the Hartcliffe and Withywood area of Bristol. This is one of the most deprived areas in the UK. The young people gained a real knowledge of the issues involved through visits to public spaces, workshops and field research. They were the clients for the scheme and made key creative decisions throughout its progress.

Another example of a networking strategy to produce educational change across a community is the 'school led community revitalization' programme that is, at time of writing, happening in 13 rural communities in New Mexico.

The New Mexico Rural Revitalization Initiative (NMRRI) is a school-led recovery effort for rural communities and schools suffering from the current degeneration of rural areas. This regenerative methodology was developed in Australia and has proven very successful in revitalizing rural schools and communities economically, socially, culturally and environmentally.

In many parts of the world, the largest human migration in history from rural to urban areas is leading to the disintegration of rural communities. People who live in these areas find much to value in the rural environment. But with declining employment and school enrolment, rural areas are 'drying up' and once the school closes the community dies.

Schools in rural communities are often the largest employers, have the best brick and mortar facilities (often underutilized) and have the most highly developed infrastructure. In addition, they possess the energy and creativity of the young people of the community.

This initiative establishes the school as the driving force behind a local revitalization movement that simultaneously involves and acts as an educational opportunity for the students. In conferences and meetings, using various facilitation, mediating and team-building techniques, the NMRRI unites the school and community in an exploration of the resources of the area. By positively reframing 'what we don't have' into 'what we do have', the school and community focus on one or more specific project areas that will improve quality of life for the school/community. This is the first step to positive change that will reposition the school as the fulcrum for the revitalization of the community. The NMRRI supports the initiation of projects chosen by the communities by facilitating a discovery process where community leaders of all ages and from many organizations and institutions, including the school, can come together to learn how the entire community can better meet the educational needs of that unique community. This can involve actions and projects that would not normally be perceived as educational activities in the traditional sense.

The progress in the revitalization process is seen as being socially, economically and educationally remarkable. This networking has transformed the educational process in these small communities in as little as three months. To support this approach to community education, an online forum for networking, communication and problem solving has been initiated to assist efforts in future funding.

Strategies to support community action

There is a range of approaches used in both schools and communities that provides structured and safe spaces that can shift the mindset of schools and bring the community to the table.

Open Space technology

Open Space technology was created in the mid-1980s by organizational consultant Harrison Owen (1997) when he discovered that people attending his conferences loved the coffee breaks better than the formal presentations and plenary sessions. He had also lived in Africa and used these insights to create a new form of conferencing.

In Open Space meetings, events and organizations, participants create and manage their own agenda around a central theme of strategic importance. Open Space conferences therefore have no keynote speakers, no pre-announced schedules of workshops and no panel discussions. The participants create the event and become their own and others' teacher, leader and learner. Anyone who wants to initiate a discussion or activity writes it down on a large sheet of paper in big letters and then stands up and announces it to the group. Proposed topics for discussion are posted and participants create their own schedule for the event.

Open Space is chaotic, productive and fun. No one is in control and everyone is. Simple ground rules help to keep the space working.

World café

The world café works on the principle of 'if you change the conversation you change the future'. It simulates 'café conversations' and is designed on the principle that people already have the wisdom and creativity they need to confront even the most difficult challenges (Brown and Isaacs, 2005). The process is simple but can achieve surprising results. It involves generating a web of conversations, in a hospitable space, where questions that matter are placed 'on the table'. Connections are made between conversations by people being encouraged to move between tables to connect thinking and learning, and to continue to ask questions. Collective knowledge is then made visible as the group moves to action.

Collaborative problem solving

This is a tool developed by Wheatley and Crinean (2004) and involves a five-stage process in order to move a group through collaborative problem solving. The five stages are:

- Cooling and quieting: bringing people into a circle to tell their story and develop a richer appreciation of the problem.

- Enriching and fruitful opposition: move to a square table and literally 'take sides', with each side responsible for developing its position in depth.

- Magnetizing resources: using opposites to generate resource. Move into a half-circle to indicate that 'we are only half-way there'. The blank space – the other half of the circle – is used to generate questions 'Who else is out there?', 'What else do we need?', 'What are we blind to and can't yet see?', 'What other perspectives do we need?'.

- Precise destroying: a focus on what needs to be destroyed – outmoded beliefs and practice, policies that are not working, individuals who refuse to change. In order to act with precision and discipline, the group moves into a triangle with a flip chart at the apex.

- Intelligent action: a focus on commitment and team work using the more familiar processes of action planning, strategy setting and project planning.

Storytelling

Within communities, shared stories can be a powerful mobilizing force. They function to emphasize what people care about, what they share and who they are. Around a school they function to develop a shared narrative of 'what we love about living and working around here' and 'what we would love to change'. Craig and O'Leary (2005) believe in the power of stories to build the belief that communities can make a difference:

> Amid the complexities of everyday interaction, stories help to anchor communities, serving as emotive aide memoires as to what communities hold dear, hold in common or aspire to achieve. (page 18)

They go on to point out that, in the past, storytelling was often a responsibility given to others – faith leaders, politicians or experts – who told the stories about our lives and the challenges we face. Today our faith in others to tell our stories is declining. One of the roles of schools is to communicate with local people, to help positive stories about local communities to develop and spread in order to build a sense of self and community efficacy and empowerment. Stories help to develop the community's belief that the future is not predetermined and they can make a difference.

This will all depend on whether or not organizations in positions of power and control are prepared to listen to communities, engage in these conversations and enable collective action and decision making to take place. School can help communities to become better storytellers, and the power of conversation is outlined in Chapter 6.

Each of these processes is characterized by the same principles. The whole community is brought into the room, and there is a collective agreement that the answers lie in the room and all contributions are equally valid. A strategic question forms the focus. There is no one leader of the process, no one right answer and no preconceived outcome. It is in these spaces that communities and organizations can meet to find a way of taking action together.

These processes and others have been used in the community leadership network at NCSL and it is interesting that those individuals who are rooted in organizational meetings, agendas and 'getting on with it' can be frustrated and feel uncomfortable, while community members recognize the invitational and open-ended nature of the process and are sometimes more prepared to trust it. Both groups need guiding through the process.

In generating authentic school–community engagement we are attempting to connect two worlds, with distinct cultures, traditions and ways of working. These insider–outsider relationships, that connect community action and school development, are hard to craft. The Institute for Educational Leadership (IfEL) has worked with community organizations and schools to address this question and to ask 'Can the two worlds ever connect?'(IfEL, 2001).

Some of the issues they identified are:

Issue I: Organizational structures
School

    Publicly funded

    Complex, hierarchical and powerful with vertical organizing structures

    Staff have specific roles and functions

    Formal selection to be included, outcome depends on training and expertise.

Community

    Small and fluid

    Non-hierarchical

    Lateral organizing structures

    Short-term funding

    Involvement comes from agency and networks.

This leads to:

    Issues of communication; who do we talk to?

    Issues of practice; how do they do things over there?

Issue II: Leadership
School

    Based on authority

    Primarily focused on a leading single institution

    Single person – highly accountable.

Community

    Open-ended opportunities for leadership

    Emerges rather than conferred

    Changes

    Shared accountability.

This leads to:

    Lack of ability to recognize the legitimacy of both types of leadership.

Issue III: Perspectives on the role of schools and schooling

School

   Performance measured by test results has led to an emphasis on standards and classroom-based practice

   Tight focus on 'the basics'.

Community

   Broader role for school in human development

   Emphasize need for the building of trusting relationships.

This leads to:

   An inability to agree a core purpose of schooling which brings the school and the community together.

Issue IV: Power, race and class

Schools

   A focus on institutional power based on size, resources and authority

   External relationships are valued when partners bring resources into the school – partners with 'clout'.

Community

   See people as the main source of power

   Wealth is defined as hard work and motivation of residents.

This leads to:

   A tension on sources of power: both institutional and people power are necessary. Schools can focus on the larger partners and ignore small groups of self-organized citizens. Because they do not bring obvious substantial resources they are often not 'courted' by the school.

Issue V: Collaboration and conflict

Schools

   Collaborations are organized and understood

   Conflict is minimized to avoid 'time wasting'.

Community

   Collaborations are fluid and changing

   Conflict is encouraged as a necessary element in consensus making.

This leads to:

> A misunderstanding of collaboration and conflict. Schools can see the latter as a sign of breakdown and retreat from it, whereas communities can see it as a necessary part of the process and expect and embrace it.

The challenge of providing environments to connect these worlds has been explored in the NCSL community leadership network, and findings are similar. These networks involve schools, communities and other agencies working together across a locality. Leadership of the network came from different places, within the school and within the community.

Participants in these networks reflected on their learning over the year and defined the following:

- Networks are diverse and each is unique, it is unhelpful and difficult to define what a community leadership network is.
- Clarity of purpose is essential for success. What do we want to achieve? What will engage us all in common purpose?
- Go with passion – it will sustain you through the tough times. There is a danger that networks feel they have to follow a government agenda rather than what genuinely motivates them.
- Build in time for review. How clear are we about what success looks like? Because networks are complex and success may not be as expected, it is important to be clear about what the network really wants to achieve and what some of the indicators are that it is getting there.
- Balance thinking and doing. Some network participants are disposed to move to action very quickly, others want to develop the strategic direction and resist unfocused action. This can be a tension.
- Good interpersonal relationships are crucial. Do we genuinely listen to and respect each other. Do we take time to understand each other's realities? How well do we share information?
- Networks go through peaks and troughs – expect them and do not be discouraged by the troughs.
- Networks need some key movers and shakers. How do we identify these and make sure the role is shared?

One of the key actions taken by one of the networks in that project was to recruit and develop 'community champions' from within the community, to bridge the gap between the community and educational opportunities. This was confirmed as the right approach when a local resident commented, 'we want some gutsy locals, not a bunch of professionals':

> You don't need to create community activists, they're already out there. You need to identify them and work with them. (Shelley, 2005, page 7)

It is interesting to note that in recruiting these champions, adverts, mailings and flyers attracted not one applicant. A member of the network involved in community work invited one of the key stakeholders from the community in to help. This person had daily contacts in the community and used her own connections to recruit 16 people.

This network was clear on the dos and don'ts of building relationships between schools and communities. They had learned these through practice but they bear a real resemblance to the principles of mutual assistance and community coalition building.

Do

Involve the community from the beginning to avoid 'doing to'.

Initiate action based on real, rather than perceived, need.

Use word of mouth as communication.

Take time to build ownership – there is no room for conflicting agendas.

Engage in small-scale activity that allows for reflection, learning and risk taking.

Use local people to resource the network – local caterers, transport for events and so on.

Develop and employ local community members as community champions.

Don't

Be hasty in building relationships – the speed will be dictated by ensuring a firm foundation of relationships. (NCSL, 2005b, page 6)

Where next?

Collaborative empowerment – building new relationships

Schools and the public sector are adept at strategic planning and organizational improvement. This leads to sector improvement. Community empowerment processes promote systematic societal change. The W.K. Kellogg Foundation (2000) has used the phrase 'collaborative empowerment' to describe the process of self-determination which emerges when mutually respectful relationships are formed between community- and neighbourhood-based organizations and larger public, private and not-for-profit-based organizations.

The principles of collaborative empowerment include:

- Local communities can solve local problems.
- The entire community must be involved.
- Resources can be found and developed at local level.

- Consensus is used to reach desired outcomes.
- Root causes of issues and underlying values are the focus.
- Diversity in the coalition makes for richness in resources and perspectives on the difficult problems.

  (W.K. Kellogg Foundation and the Healthcare Forum, 2000)

In order to connect we need to move into relationships that feel different. Schools as organizations are generally characterized by contractual relationships: staff are employed, the school has targets to meet and students have learning 'contracts' to abide by. Communities tend to be held together by predominantly social relationships: they are more fluid, less determined (at least on paper) and generated from within the community, not imposed from without by a third party. Jonathan Sacks has coined a new relationship that needs to be built to connect civil society – that of the 'covenantal relationship'. These relationships are moral, brought about by people who have the knowledge that what they do and what they are makes a difference to those around them.

It appears that caring for one another is a natural dynamic in a community. The covenantal relationship described by Sacks may well be governed by altruism. Schaeffer suggests that caring increases (and thus covenantal relationships will be strengthened) when our meanings and desires 'become a source for meaning in others' (1996, page 8). As these communities develop, so people have a desire to see others achieve their work. Many would argue that something of this sort is at the heart of most schools' mission statements: 'to help every child achieve their potential', 'to enable every child to become the best they can be'. By engaging more authentically with communities where self- and community actualization is a goal, one could argue that schools will be more able to achieve this goal within the organization.

Sacks asserts that:

> We know that schools fail without the support of families. We know that families fail without the support of communities. We know that communities fail without neighbourly virtues and the obligations that flow from fellow feeling. Civil society rests on moral relationships. (Sacks, 2000, page 268)

Margaret Wheatley, who has studied communities and organizations as living human systems, is clear that creating a clear sense of collective purpose will provide an anchor for individuals and organizations to rally around. This enables individuals to see their own contribution more clearly:

> Problematic behaviours disappear when a community knows its heart, its purpose for

being together. Boundaries between self and others, who is inside and who is outside, get weaker and weaker. (Wheatley and Kellner-Rogers, 1998, page 4)

She notices that the questions we need to answer – 'Who are we?' and 'What matters?' – are happening around kitchen tables, water coolers and in restaurants but rarely publicly:

When we don't answer these questions as a community, when we have no agreement about why we belong together, the institutions we create to serve us become battle grounds and serve no one. In the absence of these agreements, our instinct of community leads us to a community of 'me' not a community of 'we'. (Wheatley and Kellner-Rogers, 1998, pages 4–5)

Schools can learn from the actions of the community in order to help forge these agreements which will be on mutual terms and for mutual benefit.

Table 9.1 shows a hypothetical model of the movement from bonding to bridging as schools move from being exclusive institutions at Stage 1 to a community-based, fully inclusive approach at Stage 4. Such a diagram inevitably creates artificial polarization and categorization. However, there is a strong possibility that most schools would be able to recognize themselves as being predominantly at one stage. Although this book is explicitly committed to the idea that educational provision should be deliberately moving from being exclusive to being inclusive – changing the emphasis from 'me' to 'we'; moving from the European model of 'I think therefore I can' to the African concept, derived from *Ubantu* of 'I can because we are'.

Very few schools will be at Stage 1 these days. The principles and practice of the extended schools movement have ensured that most schools are in Stage 2. Special schools and Early Years provision have always operated on the boundaries of Stages 2 and 3 for most of the categories identified in the table. Stage 4 is highly hypothetical and it may well be that one of the great challenges for school and community leaders is to develop local scenarios for the future of education in the community.

Writing in 1915, Dewey argued:

The role of the community in making the school vital is just as important as the role of the school itself. For in a community where schools are looked upon as isolated institutions, as a necessary convention, the school will remain largely so in spite of the most skilful methods of teaching. But a community that demands something visible from its schools, that recognises the part they play in the welfare of the whole … Such a community will have social schools, and whatever its recourses, it will have schools that develop community spirit and interests. (cited in Skilbeck, 1970, page 125)

Table 9.1 School engagement and connectivity

	Stage 1	Stage 2	Stage 3	Stage 4
	Leadership focused on school improvement and management	Leadership involvement with community initiatives	Leadership focused on community renewal and social activism	Leadership distributed across the community
	Parents involved by invitation	Active contributions sought from parents	Families as partners in education	Families as primary educators
	Restricted definition of the curriculum	Inclusive curriculum involving 'knowledge-creators'	Negotiated and relevant curriculum	Community-based curriculum
	Functional engagement with other agencies	Positive co-operation with other agencies	Full integration with other agencies	'Joined-up' services
	Minimal alternative use of resources	Controlled access to school resources	School as a community resource	Educational resources across the community
	Teachers' role limited to effective pedagogy	Teachers engaged with parents and community initiatives	Teachers as social educators	Diverse educators
			The school as a centre for social and economic entrepreneurship	

Bonding — Bridging

Exclusive   Moving towards inclusion   Inclusive

(Adapted from Gelsthorpe and West-Burnham, 2003, page 27)

10 Change and complexity in communities

Introduction

In many ways this chapter serves as a synthesis of all that has gone before. It explores the nature of organizations and communities, and reflects on the process of change in order to identify criteria for successful innovation and growth. The discussion ignores much of the conventional wisdom about 'managing change', believing that phrase to be one of the great oxymorons. Instead it focuses on:

- Communities as complex adaptive systems
- Strategies to enable change in complex situations
- Principles into practice
- The politics of change
- Complexity and change: a synthesis.

Communities as complex adaptive systems

If only every human community was as logical and well ordered as a beehive! For a start there would be no need for a discussion of change – everyone would know the overarching core purpose of the community – to replicate itself – and their role within it. Ellis (2004) provides graphic examples of the efficiency of bee communities:

> As interesting and impressive as bees are individually, it is as a collective force that they most fascinate. Each bee may be a tiny fraction of the hive, but each one plays its part. The collective life of the hive enables it not just to thrive but to grow, with groups of bees breaking off, or swarming, to create new colonies. (page 34)

From the moment she [the worker bee] is born to the moment she dies, she performs a series of widely differing tasks: cleaning cells; tending and feeding the larvae and pupae; building and repairing the honeycomb and nest; receiving nectar from foraging bees and further processing it into honey; receiving and packing pollen into the cells; ventilating the hive to keep it at the right temperature by flapping her wings; and guarding the entrance to the hive. Then about half-way through her life, going out to forage flowers; bringing back nectar and pollen and reporting good finds to the hive; making honey; eating some honey herself; and going out again to forage some more. (page 37)

For better or ill, human societies appear to lack the uniformity, discipline and clarity of the hive. For all its sophistication, the hive is, fundamentally, a simple society. Human society, by contrast, has an almost infinite number of permutations, networks and relationships. However, this apparent complexity is deceptive. Think of any large city; it is the most astonishing expression of an enormous number of interactions that are virtually impossible to manage centrally. Yet most cities function very well: people travel, work, are fed, go shopping, buy newspapers and communicate in numerous ways all without central direction. In fact, cities work because they are complex adaptive systems as are beehives and virtually all forms of living organisms.

Morrison (2002) provides a powerful summary of schools as complex adaptive systems:

- they require organization and have distinguishing structures and features that change over time;
- they are dynamical and unpredictable organizations;
- they are nonlinear organizations: causes do not always straightforwardly produce effects … ;
- small changes can have massive effects;
- they are complex, complicated and constantly changing;
- they are a human service and rely on people;
- relationships are highly important to their work;
- they have to adapt in response to macro- and micro-societal change;
- the environments (external and internal) in which they operate are largely unpredictable and mutable;
- they have to maintain 'relative autonomy' from the wider society;
- they exert pressure on their members;
- they have a range of methods of communication and rely on communication and effective networking;
- the synergy of their several parts is greater than any individual or smaller combination of individuals;
- new properties emerge at every level of the organization … ;
- they are learning organizations; they have a proclivity to instability and operate at the edge of chaos. (pages 26–27)

Exactly the same principles can be applied to any human grouping – notably a community. Given such complexity it becomes nonsense to talk about 'managing' change in the same way that it is impossible to manage a city. Bringing about change is to engage with the characteristics of a complex adaptive system; not to try and impose an external logic, assume causality and predictability and work through certainty and order, but rather recognize that:

> A complex system comprises independent elements (which themselves might be made up of complex systems) which interact and give rise to organized behaviour in the systems as a whole. Order is not totally predetermined and fixed, but the universe (however defined) is creative, emergent (through iteration, learning and recursion), evolutionary and changing, transformative and turbulent. Order emerges in complex systems that are founded on simple rules for interacting organisms; life is holistic and profoundly unpredictable. (Morrison, 2002, page 9)

Fundamental to the concept of complex adaptive systems is the theory of emergence. Johnson (2001) captures the essence of emergence:

> The forms of emergent behaviour that we'll examine … show the distinctive quality of growing smarter over time, and of responding to the specific and changing needs of their environment. (page 20)

> … we have stopped analyzing emergence and started creating it. We began building self-organizing systems into our software applications, our video games, our art, our music. We built emergent systems to recommend new books, recognize our voices, or find mates. For as long as complex organisms have been alive, they have lived under the laws of self-organization, but in recent years our day-to-day life has become overrun with artificial emergence: systems build with a conscious understanding of what emergence is, systems designed to exploit those laws … . (page 21)

In essence, schools and the communities they serve are in a perpetual state of growth, change and development. Sometimes it is possible to point to a clear and explicit source for a change, for example a change in government policy, but the impact of that policy, the way it is interpreted and applied, and the impact it has are subject to a wide range of interconnected variables that make it impossible to have confidence that the desired outcomes will result from a specific initiative. Although, possibly, we can begin to explore strategies that are actively engaged with creating desired situations, it has to be recognized that there are numerous variables that will influence the outcome. Think of any journey that you do on a regular basis – perhaps the drive to work. On the one hand there is a number of givens – starting and finishing points, roundabouts, traffic lights and so on. Then think of the variables that influence the success of your journey – starting time, time of year, weather, accidents, breakdowns, roadworks and the sheer capriciousness of your fellow travellers. The roads are chaotic, our journeys are complex even though there are so many given factors.

So it is with change in schools and communities. That which is predictable is always subject to a range of factors that cannot be managed. We learn to accommodate the vagaries of our journey; we may also need to learn to think of change in schools and communities in a different way.

Wise policy makers have long learned that, in spite of the integrity of their research, the clarity of their definitions and formulations, the authority of their pronouncements and the detail of their strategy, there will be no guarantee that the system will actually change. The logic of strategy is almost always challenged by the complexity of organizations and communities. The movement from bonding to bridging – which is central to this section of the book – cannot be mandated; it is not amenable to logic and will not result from a strategic plan.

Capra (2002) captures the tensions involved in changing organizations and communities:

> According to the systems view of life, the spontaneous emergence of order and the dynamics of structural coupling, which results in the continual structural changes that are characteristic of all living systems, are the basic phenomena underlying the process of learning. Moreover, we have seen that the creation of knowledge in social networks is a key characteristic of the dynamics of culture. (page 88)

> The experience of the critical instability that precedes the emergence of novelty may involve uncertainty, fear, confusion or self-doubt. Experienced leaders recognize these emotions as integral parts of the whole dynamic and create a climate of trust and mutual support. (page108)

> During the change process some of the old structures may fall apart, but if the supportive climate and the feedback loops in the network of communication persist, new and more meaningful structures are likely to emerge. When that happens, people often feel a sense of wonder and elation, and now the leader's role is to acknowledge these emotions and provide opportunities for celebration. (page 108)

The changes associated with the movement from bonding to bridging require more than an extension of the logic of managing an organization; they involve a fundamental rethinking of how communities work as systems, how they adapt and how they emerge.

Strategies to enable change in complex situations

Change does not come about because of a moral imperative, systematic planning or a brute sanity. This section will explore strategies to build on the idea of schools and communities as complex adaptive systems and change as emergence. Conventional models of change management will not work in this context, so it is necessary to introduce two alternative perspectives. First, Gladwell's (2000) concept of the 'tipping point' and, second, Kelley's (2005) strategies for innovation.

In *The Tipping Point*, Gladwell argues that social change is often the cumulative result of small changes:

> We need to prepare ourselves for the possibility that sometimes big changes follow from small events, and that sometimes these changes can happen very quickly.
>
> This possibility of sudden change is at the center of the ideal of the Tipping Point and might well be the hardest of all to accept. ... The Tipping Point is the moment of critical mass, the threshold, the boiling point. (pages 11–12)

In essence, change works as a geometric progression – one small event can lead to significant social change, for example:

> All epidemics have Tipping Points. Jonathon Crane, a sociologist at the University of Illinois, has looked at the effect the number of role models in a community – the professionals, managers, teachers whom the Census Bureau has defined as 'high status' – has on the lives of teenagers in the same neighborhood. He found little difference in pregnancy rates or school drop-out rates in neighborhoods between 40 and 5 percent of high status workers. But when the number of professionals dropped below 5 percent, the problems exploded. (pages 12–13)

Thus, changing a community may be more a matter of initiating an epidemic than producing a business plan.

Gladwell argues that creating an epidemic is the result of observing three roles:

- the Law of the Few;
- the Stickiness Factor;
- the Power of Context.

The law of the Few relates to individuals who are pivotal to achieving the tipping point. Gladwell characterizes them as:

Connectors: people with rich and sophisticated networks of friends, contacts, acquaintances and reference groups.

Mavens: Maven is a Yiddish word and it means one who accumulates knowledge, a person who has access to information, in essence, an intelligence gatherer.

Salesmen [sic]: people with the ability to persuade and influence, highly skilled communicators who work through compelling interactions.

These characteristics are not particularly distinctive or unique – there are clear echoes of many of the characteristics of effective leaders discussed in Chapter 9. However, it is when they are combined in the context of social change that they become especially potent. What enhances the power of these characteristics in Gladwell's model is that they are linked with his other two roles.

The Stickiness Factor refers to the nature of the message carried by 'the Few':

And the specific quality that a message needs to be successful is the quality of 'stickiness'. Is the message – or the food, or the movie, or the product – memorable? Is it so memorable, in fact, that it can create change, that it can spur someone to action? (Gladwell, 2000, page 92)

Stickiness refers to the extent a message is relevant, meaningful, and significant and valued.

The third element, the Power of Context, is particularly relevant to the main themes of this book. Context refers to the environments in which we live and work. Gladwell cites a number of cases to demonstrate that crime, for example, can be prevented by improving the physical appearance of a particular location:

Once you understand that context matters, however, that specific and relatively small elements in the environment can serve as Tipping Points, that defeatism is turned upside down. Environmental Tipping Points are things that we can change: we can fix broken windows and clean up graffiti and change the signals that invite crime in the first place. Crime can be more than understood. It can be prevented. (page 167)

Combine the Few with Stickiness and Context and it becomes possible to explore a strategy that recognizes that change in society, communities and organizations is the result of a complex interaction of variables. Although Gladwell's work has been subjected to substantial academic critiques (it is not academic sociology) there is anecdotal power to his model. Central to his theoretical framework is a mathematical model of how epidemics work; the movement from a medical to a social model seems to explain how ideas and products can behave. It takes just one person to start a 'flu' epidemic – in social terms:

Merely by manipulating the size of a group, we can dramatically improve its receptivity to new ideas. By tinkering with the presentation of information, we can significantly improve its stickiness. Simply by finding and reaching those few special people who hold so much social power, we can shape the course of social epidemics. In the end, Tipping Points are a reaffirmation of the potential for change and the power of intelligent action. Look at the world around you. It may seem like an immovable, implacable place. It is not. With the slightest push – in just the right place – it can be tipped. (Gladwell, 2000, page 259)

Many of the principles of Gladwell's model can be found in the work of Kelley (2005). Kelley's focus is on innovation in organizations but it can be argued that his principles can be applied to communities of any type. Kelley has identified ten 'personas', ideal types who make specific contributions to innovation.

The learning personas

Individuals and organizations need to constantly gather new sources of information in order to expand their knowledge and grow, so the first three personas are *learning roles* ...

1. The anthropologist brings new learning and insights into the organization by observing human behavior and developing a deep understanding of how people interact physically and emotionally with products, services and spaces ...

2. The experimenter prototypes new ideas continuously, learning by a process of enlightened trial and error ...

3. The cross-pollinator explores other industries and cultures, then translates those findings and revelations to fit the unique needs of your enterprise.

The organizing personas

The next three personas are *organizing roles*, played by individuals who are savvy about the often counterintuitive process of how organizations move ideas forward ...

4. The hurdler knows the path to innovation is strewn with obstacles and develops a knack for overcoming or outsmarting those roadblocks ...

5. The collaborator helps bring eclectic groups together, and often leads from the middle of the pack to create new combinations and multidisciplinary solutions ...

6. The director not only gathers together a talented cast and crew but also helps to spark their creative talents ...

The building personas

The four remaining personas are *building roles* that apply insights from the learning roles and channel the empowerment from the organizing roles to make innovation happen ...

7. The experienced architect designs compelling experiences that go beyond mere functionality to connect at a deeper level with customers' latent or expressed needs …

8. The set designer creates a stage on which innovation team members can do their best work, transforming physical environments into powerful tools to influence behavior and attitude …

9. The caregiver builds on the metaphor of a health care professional to deliver customer care in a manner that goes beyond mere service …

10. The storyteller builds both internal morale and external awareness through compelling narratives that communicate a fundamental human value or reinforce a specific cultural trait … (pages 8–12)

Readers will very quickly recognize Kelley's approach – there are numerous formulations available to classify community, organizational and team 'types'. Kelley's approach is useful because it has an explicit focus on innovation and that may be a more powerful mental model in this context than change.

Kelley is very careful to insist that 'A persona is not about your predetermined business DNA' (page 13). Anyone can take on any of these roles, most people will be able to work with several persona and they can change over time. What Kelley has to say about the organization can apply equally to elements within the school, the school itself and the wider community it serves:

> Innovation doesn't happen on its own, but with the right team, you're up to the challenge. So find new paths of learning with the Anthropologist, the Experimenter, and the Cross-Pollinator. Organize for innovation with the Hurdler, the Collaborator, and the Director. Ask the Set Designer to help build your stage, and bring on the Experience Architect, the Caregiver, and the Storyteller to wow your audience. Innovation doesn't just turn companies around. It becomes a way of life. It's fun. It's invigorating. It works. With all ten personas on your side, you can drive creativity through the whole organization and build your own unique culture of innovation. (page 266)

In the final analysis, change and innovation are all about perception. Any community is the result of a mass of competing or confirming perceptions. If we are to secure change then we have to work with and through people, and that means focusing on relationships. What Gladwell and Kelley offer are ways of recognizing and then working with the complexity of multiple perceptions: their approach is neither cynical nor manipulative but rather pragmatic; recognizing that people are open to influence and persuasion and that moral integrity may not be enough.

Principles into practice

Frequent reference has already been made to Robert Putnam's (2000) seminal work *Bowling Alone*. In many ways it is the inspiration for much of the work that we are engaged in. The publication of *Bowling Alone* led to a great deal of debate and discussion about the issue of building social capital. More importantly, it led to Putnam learning about many community-based initiatives. Some of these were published in 2003 as *Better Together*. What follows is a summary of the successful strategies that emerged from the case studies in *Better Together*. The key message is a very simple one:

> … virtually no one sets out to 'build social capital'. Protagonists in our stories set out to raise farm incomes in Mississippi or help poor kids in Philadelphia or build parks in Portland or save souls in Los Angeles. However, they saw that achieving their substantive objectives would be easier (or perhaps would only be possible) if they strengthened and then exploited social networks. Thus, building social capital was an essential part of their strategy. Indeed, what distinguishes our cases from other efforts to organize unions, run large companies, build churches, or improve reading skills is that the protagonists here understand and emphasize the centrality of relationships and interpersonal connections. (page 269)

The other factors are, in no order of priority:

- Careful analysis of the 'structural conditions', those factors that are available to support an initiative. For example, the availability of resources from a range of sources and the use of existing policies and strategies to underpin a community initiative.

- The use of federation, 'nesting' smaller groups within larger groups to enhance a sense of belonging and commitment, and to foster personal relationships.

- Fostering social ties and interdependence by developing an overarching and shared sense of belonging through common purpose and shared values.

- Recognizing the need for ownership through the development and respect for people's own stories, build the capacity for dialogue through valuing personal and collective narratives.

- Building multi-stranded networks of shared interest and common concern that utilize a wide range of communication technologies.

- 'Reweaving social webs will depend in part on the efforts of dedicated local leaders who choose to pursue their goals … through the sometimes slow, frequently fractious, and profoundly transformative route of social capital building. But reweaving will also depend on our ability to create new spaces for recognition, reconnection, conversation and debate.' (Putnam, 2003, page 294)

What is very clear from Putnam's studies is that community action is almost invariably in response to a real and practical need; it is often very modest in its aspirations and success is almost directly correlated with the depth and quality of human interaction. To these factors may be added a range of qualities and skills that can be described as leadership, but might also be seen as political awareness.

The politics of change

Change in organizations and communities is rarely perceived as a political process. Yet one of the defining characteristics of social capital is 'civic engagement' (see page 32). Change and innovation usually involve a rethinking of roles and values, the redeployment of resources and a reorientation of power and authority. In many ways this is a perfect description of the political process. In her study of community initiatives and political action, Wainwright (2003) identifies a number of factors that support the movement towards participatory democracy:

> First, if any form of participatory democracy is to achieve legitimacy as a source of power over decisions concerning the government of a locality, it needs to be open at its foundations to everyone affected by such decisions – even if only a minority participate.
>
> Second, there need to be mutually agreed and openly negotiated rules.
>
> A third condition, always difficult to preserve, is the autonomy of the participatory process form the state. Not that it can be entirely separate …
>
> … a fourth condition: the genuine sharing of knowledge. We have seen how a process of democratisation through which users and service workers can contribute their knowledge to improving services is an unexplored strategy for public service reform … A further basic condition then, is that real resources must be at stake, resources which could make a positive difference to the livers of the community.
>
> Finally, there's no doubt that the feasibility and legitimacy of the participatory process is enormously enhanced by the existence and electoral success of a party that believes in it. (pages 188–189)

It could be argued that embarking on a change process without a political perspective is naïve and ignores the context in which most communities work – which is primarily about power, control over resources and accountability. It is also worth stating that schools and communities operate within a democracy and the broad principles of democratic processes should be embedded in all social structures and strategies:

> But while democracy has evident defects, it also possesses two great attributes. The first is that it is the only political system which contains the potential for its own improvement. We can overthrow our representatives without having to kill them. To a lesser extent, we can affect their behaviour while they remain in office. Democracy can be understood as a self-refining experiment in collective action.

The second is that democracy has the potential to be politically engaging. The more politically active citizens become, the more they are able to affect the way the state is run. The more success they encounter in changing the state, the more likely they are to remain politically active. (Monbiot, 2004, pages 45–46)

Complexity and change: a synthesis

By way of a conclusion to this chapter it is appropriate to bring together all of the various elements that have been explored to offer an, at best, emergent model of the principles that might inform the change process:

1. Change is the norm; it is impossible not to be changing. Organizations and communities are complex adaptive systems in constant interaction.
2. Change can be influenced by individuals who bring specific skills, strategies and qualities to the change process. Their influence can be disproportionate to their number.
3. Communication is fundamental to successful change; open, sophisticated networks engaging in rich conversations and dialogue are elemental to securing understanding and commitment.
4. Change is most likely to be successful if it is focused on relevant, real, local, significant, short-term and attainable projects.
5. Innovation requires the development and deployment of a range of behaviours that everyone can develop.
6. Change requires recognition of the political context, building networks and coalitions and bargaining for resources.
7. Above all, successful change is about common purpose, shared values and a commitment to improvement.

11 Monitoring, review and evaluation

The purpose of this chapter is to provide a resource to support monitoring, review and evaluation processes for those involved in all the different components of the developing relationship between schools and the community. The chapter is presented as a series of questions grouped according to the main themes of the book. It is hoped that these questions will serve as a stimulus to support the design of the range of instruments in order to support the crucial task of obtaining feedback.

There are multiple definitions of the procedures outlined in the title of this chapter. The authors would suggest the following broad definitions:

Monitoring: Short-term, often quantitative, surveys which provide evidence that activity is actually taking place or satisfaction surveys, for example of an in-service event.

Review: (a) A formative analysis by a team or as the result of questioning or interviews of the extent to which a service or project is meeting its stated outcomes.

(b) A reflection on personal effectiveness or an analysis of the data in order to inform future action.

Evaluation: A summative process to judge the extent to which a service or project has actually achieved its stated outcomes and has made an impact.

Monitoring and review are essentially developmental processes designed to inform future action. They are fundamental to effective leadership, project management and action learning approaches. Evaluation provides the basis for responding to different levels of accountability and can be used to demonstrate impact.

Although the parallels are inappropriate and dangerous, measuring the impact of community engagement is similar to evaluating a holiday. There is a significant range of factors that can be measured against explicit quantitative criteria (flights on time, the hotel looking as it did in the brochure) but the overall impact of a holiday will be subject to a wide range of complex interacting variables that give rise to a subjective, often emotional, response. Such responses are valid and appropriate but in the context of this book need to be understood in a broader context which legitimates a learning experience according to a range of criteria. The ability to demonstrate change is contingent on the generation of criteria that can be used to inform the measurement of relative degrees of change which can be attributed to a specific variable or a combination of variables. In the context of developing community-based strategies it is necessary to explore the components of the potential impact of the activity.

Demonstrating impact is essential in order to:

- justify the investment of time, effort and funds;
- demonstrate relevance and credibility;
- meet the requirements of funding agencies;
- demonstrate reliability, validity and so replicability;
- identify the extent to which participants achieved intended outcomes.

There is a substantial number of ways to measure impact, all of which relate to a range of potential outcomes:

- inputs, events, activities;
- engagement with people;
- emotional responses;
- changes in knowledge, qualities, skills;
- changes in practice;
- improvement in performance.

The further down this list the more difficult it becomes to provide directly attributable evidence of impact on learning outcomes. The first two levels can be objectively monitored: did the individual attend and participate in the event? The second two levels are more complex but can still be defined and identified – especially when working in a novel or distinctive environment. It is the other levels that are most problematic because of the troubles in developing any logical model of causality that can attribute changes in practice and performance to a specific experience.

In order to move beyond high satisfaction ratings in terms of novelty, a sense of privilege, recognition and the 'X' factor, it is necessary to identify a range of strategies that will allow a focus on actual impact rather than cosmetic satisfaction. This would imply the following data being available (as relevant):

- personal history and motivation;
- contextual data, for example school self-evaluation;

- clarification of purpose/focus;
- rationale for the activity;
- learning outcomes, success criteria;
- pre-/post-questionnaire, diagnostic;
- pre-/post-360° appraisals;
- longitudinal studies.

Measurement might be facilitated by:

- the development of a weighted taxonomy of indicators of school or project success;
- the creation of models of value added which would facilitate comparative analysis;
- detailed case studies of schools in specific circumstances to build up a profile of indicators;
- collecting narratives from stakeholders and protagonists before and after a project and using these to construct a comparative taxonomy;
- developing models, which would allow the measurement of per capita impact;
- the use of some of the above to establish international benchmarks to facilitate relative progress to be judged;
- the development of 'indicators of confidence'.

The model in Figure 11.1 attempts to summarize the key components of this discussion. The central proposition is that impact is a direct function of the other factors, the clearer the definition of each component the more possible it will be to make a valid judgement about impact. However, each element is subject to a range of variables and the interaction between each element is a crucial variable in itself.

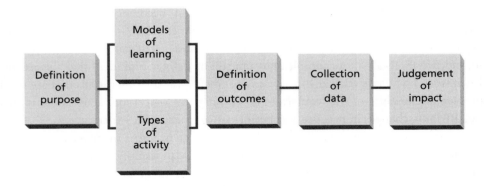

Figure 11.1 Measuring impact

There are many complex intervening variables and it would require a highly sophisticated causal analysis to isolate the precise impact of professional development except where there is a direct transposition of a specific strategy from one school to another. However, there may be a case to argue that such transfer will always be problematic because of the very different contextual factors prevailing.

The key factors that will influence relative perceptions of impact might include:

- moral, political and philosophical stances (normative versus interpretive);
- ideological perspectives on training and development (efficiency versus effectiveness; idiographic versus nomothetic);
- relative status (perceived significance and relevance);
- competing linguistic positions (for example, definitions of leadership);
- hygiene factors (as per Herzberg, 1966);
- social interaction and engagement – the Hawthorne effect;
- alternative epistemological perspectives (quantitative versus qualitative; objective versus subjective; scientific versus ethnographic).

There is a case to be made that the simulation, revitalization and refreshment of leaders is, in itself, a valid and legitimate activity. If it also enhances learning as part of a systematic and coherent strategy, then it is possible to be confident of impact in terms of leadership learning and development which in turn impacts school climate and so performance.

The questions set out below can be used to generate evidence in a wide variety of ways:

- as the basis for structured or semi-structured interviews;
- as an agenda for a focus group;
- in questionnaires as open questions or for structured responses using a Likert scale;
- as question to prompt a team review through discussion;
- as prompts for conversations with a mentor or coach;
- to structure personal reflection.

1. School values

1. What references are made in the school's documents to social justice, inclusion and equity?
2. To what extent have the principles of *Every Child Matters* been translated into school policy in:
   - the school aims/mission statement;
   - school policies;
   - job descriptions?

3. What has been the role and contribution of students, parents, staff and governors to the formulation of school values?

4. How does the school articulate its commitment to, and relationship with, its broader community?

5. What evidence is there of the extent to which the school is translating its principles into practice?

6. What strategies do you use to monitor, review and evaluate the extent to which the school's values are translated into the concrete experience of every student?

7. To what extent do the values of the school coincide with those of the community it serves?

8. How often are matters relating to values on the agenda of the governing body, the leadership team and staff meetings?

2. The governing body

1. Is the governing body representative of the community the school serves?

2. How often does the governing body review the school's aims?

3. Is the governing body directly involved in initiatives with the community?

4. Does the governing body actively seek members from under-represented sections of the community?

5. Has there been a resource audit of the governing body to identify knowledge, skills, networks and experience that may help the school engage with its community?

3. Community cohesion standards for schools

To what extent is the school working towards the community cohesion standards as expressed in the aims and related objectives:

I. Close the attainment and achievement gap

- Assessment arrangements enable all students to attain at the highest level possible and do not put any group of students at a substantial disadvantage.
- All staff have an equal opportunity for promotion to all levels within the school.
- The school contributes to capacity building within the community.

II. Develop common values of citizenship based on dialogue, mutual respect and acceptance of diversity

- Curriculum content contributes to an appreciation of cultural diversity, and challenges prejudice, bias and stereotype.
- The mainstream curriculum provides pupils with opportunities to learn about and become involved in the life of their communities.

- Behaviour and discipline policies and procedures reflect the commitment to developing mutual respect and acceptance of diversity.
- All staff and governors have the knowledge and understanding to provide opportunities to develop common values of citizenship based on dialogue, mutual respect and acceptance of diversity.

III. Contribute to building good community relations and challenge all types of discrimination and inequality

- The school works with the local education authority and other providers to train its staff and governors in their responsibilities under relevant legislation.
- All staff and governors have the knowledge and understanding to promote good community relations and challenge discrimination.
- The school takes positive steps to promote good community relations.
- Partnership arrangements are conducted in line with the school's equality policies.

IV. Remove the barriers to access, participation, progression, attainment and achievement

- The criteria and terms of offering a place at school, or placement at a college or work-based learning reflect the local 'catchment area' or produce a mixed intake.
- The school excludes the minimum number of students with no significant differences in exclusion rates between different social or ethnic groups.
- All students have access to the full curriculum and no one group is over-represented in vocational routes or disapplied from the National Curriculum.
- The staff profile represents the diversity of British society.
- The governing body reflects the communities it serves.
- All pupils, parents and community members have equal access to education and training provision in the local area (Home Office Community Cohesion Unit, 2004).

4. The school as a community resource

1. How do we promote and practise dialogue in more effective ways?
2. How do we develop trust?
3. How do we develop a personalized and positive learning culture?
4. How do we focus on supporting creativity and renewal?
5. How can we emphasize the importance of storytelling, play and games in learning?
6. How can we foster civic engagement, both locally and globally?
7. How can we initiate partnerships with school staff, young people, parents and the community?
8. How can we develop everyone's capacity as a student, teacher and learner?

9. How can we incorporate other ways of knowing and other cultural traditions in the way we teach and learn and our community?

10. How can we support and implement instructional, learning and community conversations throughout the school community?

5. School engagement and connectivity

Please refer to Table 9.1 on page 154. At what stage do you perceive your school to be? How would you classify your school against each of the variables used in the model?

1. The focus and nature of leadership.

2. Parental involvement and engagement.

3. The curriculum model in use.

4. The level of engagement with other agencies.

5. The school as a resource.

6. The role of the teacher.

How would you explain and justify the current stage of development of your school? What will moving to the next stage involve?

6. Bonding and bridging

Please refer to Figure 2.4 on page 34. Using the classification in the model how would you describe:

a. your school

b. the community it serves.

What are the implications of your analysis for:

a. developing strategies for your school as a community?

b. appropriate strategies to engage with your school's wider community?

7. Social capital

Consider the components of social capital listed on page 32. For each component provide a concrete example or illustration to describe the extent to which it is available to (a) your school and (b) the wider community.

Shared social norms:

a. school

b. community.

Sophisticated social networks:

   a. school

   b. community.

High levels of trust:

   a. school

   b. community.

High civic engagement:

   a. school

   b. community.

Symbols and rituals:

   a. school

   b. community.

Interdependence and reciprocity:

   a. school

   b. community.

Volunteering and community action:

   a. school

   b. community.

8. Understanding your community

How would you classify the community your school serves in *qualitative* terms? (For example, which of the following terms would you use – hope, despair, apathy, positive, creative, moribund, growing, declining, caring, aloof?)

   How would you classify you community in quantitative terms? For example:

1. What is the current and projected age profile?

2. How many births are there each year and how many of these are to single mothers?

3. What proportion of the community is retired? What is the projection for 2010, 2015?

4. How healthy is the community, for example average age at death?

5. What is the provision of doctors and dentists?

6. What are the current levels of drug abuse?

7. What are the current rates of teenage pregnancy, teenage abortion and teenage sexually transmitted diseases?

8. What are the current levels of crime?

9. How many people are in full-time permanent employment?

10. How many people are in employment but earning the minimum wage?

11. What proportion of the population are people with disabilities or with access/mobility problems?

12. What is the ethnic composition of the community? How many different languages are spoken at home? What are the main faith communities?

13. How effective is the public transport network?

14. How many different clubs, societies and voluntary organizations operate in the community?

On the basis of your qualitative perceptions and quantitative data:

What sort of community is your school serving?

Are you providing services appropriate to that community?

9. Parental and community participation in learning

1. Is there a shared definition of learning that is used across the school, shared with families, the community and other agencies?

2. In what ways are parents and carers active partners in their children's learning?

3. What use is made of the knowledge and skills available across the community?

4. Are teachers actively engaged in building a professional 'community of practice' across the schools?

5. Are there professional networks bridging primary, special, secondary, further and higher education?

6. Is professional development shared across networks?

7. Are schools open to all learners?

8. Is there a real commitment to create a learning community?

10. Leadership

1. Is there a shared understanding of the nature of leadership across the community?

2. Are the various agencies serving the community sharing their leadership development strategies and development opportunities?

3. What steps have been taken to develop leadership capacity in the following groups?

- Students
- Support staff
- Classroom teachers
- Middle leaders
- School leaders
- Governors
- Parents.

4. What evidence is there of shared and distributed leadership in the following areas?

- Leading projects
- Building teams
- Supporting innovation
- Volunteering and civic action.

5. What is being done to ensure the personal effectiveness and sustainability of all leaders?

11. Links with agencies

1. What steps are being taken to build social capital across children's services?
2. In what ways are working practices and operating procedures being integrated?
3. What work has been done to build a shared set of principles that all agencies work to?
4. What is being done to develop a shared sense of accountability?
5. How deeply embedded are the principles of *Every Child Matters*?
6. To what extent have new models of collaborative approaches been agreed?

12. Community action

1. What opportunities are there to celebrate the distinctive nature of the community?
2. What are the most significant issues and challenges facing the community? What joint steps are being taken to address them?
3. What opportunities are there for community action in the following areas?

- Literacy and numeracy
- Parenting skills
- Community service
- Cultural events
- Drug abuse
- Teenage pregnancy
- Inclusion of people with disabilities
- Environmental issues
- Political activism
- Challenging racism and sexism
- Building links with other communities – nationally and internationally.

Conclusion

Underpinning all of the issues raised so far in this chapter is one fundamental question:

> **To what extent is this community working together to secure social justice?**

This, it seems to the authors, is the most important single issue facing communities, schools and every other agency.

In the final analysis we can plan, manage, structure, organize and so on, but the essence of community comes from a shared understanding of fundamental truths that cannot be reduced to a satisfaction survey. These final quotations capture the essence of this book.

> Families are where we discover the bonds of love and trust. Schools are where we learn the collective story of which we are a part. Communities are where we are there for other people at times of need, and they for us. Congregations are where we join our prayers to those of others, making their hopes our own. Collectively they are the places where we learn to speak the language of 'We' as well as 'I'. They are where we learn moral literacy, 'habits of the heart', the give-and-take of rights and responsibilities, the grammar of reciprocity. Without them, society is too abstract to be real. Community is society with a human face. (Sacks, 2000, page xvi)

> The hope that we can learn together, teach together, be curiously impatient together, produce something together, and resist together the obstacles that prevent the flowering of our joy. In truth, from the point of view of the human condition, hope is an essential component and not an intruder. It would be a serious contradiction of what we are if, aware of our unfinishedness, we are not disposed to participate in a constant movement of search, which in its very nature is an expression of hope. Hope is a natural, possible, and necessary impetus in the context of our unfinishedness. (Freire, 2001, page 69)

References

Adonis, A. and Pollard, S. (1997) *A Class Act*, London: Penguin Books

Aldridge, S. (2006) *Social Mobility: A discussion paper*
www.strategy.gov.uk/work_areas/social_mobility

Alexander, H. and Macdonald, E. (2005) *Evaluating Policy-driven Multi-agency Partnership Working*, 11th Annual UKES Conference, Manchester

Archard, D. (2004) *Children Rights and Childhood*, 2nd edn, Abingdon: Routledge

Archard, D. (2005) Who are children?', in La Folette, H. (ed.), *The Oxford Handbook of Practical Ethics*, Oxford: Oxford University Press

Battle, M. (1997) *Reconciliation*, Cleveland, Oh: The Pilgrim Press

Blank, M.J., Berg, A. and Melaville, A. (2006) *Community Based Learning: Engaging students for success and citizenship*, Washington, DC: Coalition for Community Schools

Brown, J. and Isaacs, D., The World Café (2005) *Shaping our Futures through Conversations that Matter*, San Francisco, Calif: Berrett-Kochler

Bryk, A. and Schneider, B. (2002) *Trust in Schools*, New York: Russell Sage Foundation

Buonfino, A. and Mulgan, G. (eds) (2006) *Porcupines in Winter*, London: The Young Foundation

Cabinet Office (2006) *Leadership for Reform and Customer Focus*
www.cabinetoffice.gov.uk/workforcematters/leadership/reform/index.asp

Capra, F. (2002) *The Hidden Connections*, London: HarperCollins

Carroll, L. (1872) *Through the Looking Glass* quote taken from Partington, A. (ed.) *The Oxford Dictionary of Quotations* (1992), London: BCA

Chapman M. and Harris, A. (2004) 'Strategies for school improvement in schools facing challenging circumstances', *Educational Research*, 46(3): 219–228

Cleaver, H. (2006) 'The influence of parenting and other family relationships', in Aldgate, J., Jones, D., Rose, W. and Jeffery, C. (eds) *The Developing World of the Child*, London: Jessica Kingsley Publications

Coalition for Community Schools (2003) *Making the Difference*, www.communityschools.org

Coleman, A. (2005) *Lessons from Extended Schools*, Nottingham: NCSL

Coleman, A. (2006) *Collaborative Leadership in Extended Schools: Leading in a multi–agency environment*, Nottingham: NCSL

Collins, J. (2001) *Good to Great*, New York: HarperCollins

ContinYou.org.uk (2006) 'Share' project

Craig, J. and O'Leary, D. (2005) *The Invisible Teacher: How schools can unlock the power of community*, London: DEMOS

Craig, J., O'Leary, D. and Henehan, K. (2005) *Community Leadership: A discussion paper*, London: DEMOS

Craig, J. and Perri 6 (2004) *School's Out – Can teachers, social workers and health staff learn to live together?*, London: DEMOS

Craig, J. and Skidmore, P. (2005) *Start with People*, London: DEMOS

Davies Jones, H. (2000) *The Social Pedagogue in Western Europe – Some implications for European interprofessional care*, www.childrenuk.co.uk/

De Geus, A. (1998) *The Living Company*, London: Nicholas Brealey Publishing

De Rijke, J. (2005) 'Engaging parents through networks', in Bond, K. and Farrar, M. (eds) *What are we Learning About Community Leadership in Networks?*, Nottingham: NCSL

Decker, L.E. & Associates (1990) *Community Education: Building learning communities*, Alexandria, Va: National Community Education Association

Department for Education and Skills (2003) *Excellence and Enjoyment: A strategy for primary schools*, London: DfES

Department for Education and Skills (2004) *National Standards for Headteachers*, Nottingham: DfES Publications

Department for Education and Skills (2005a) *Every Child Matters, Change for Children: Extended schools – access to opportunities and services for all*, London: DfES

Department for Education and Skills (2005b) *Extended Schools: Access to opportunities and services for all*. A prospectus, London: DfES

Desforges, C. (2003) *The Impact of Parental Involvement, Parental Support and Family Education on Pupil Achievements and Adjustment: A literature review*, London: Department for Education and Skills Research Report: RR433

Diamond, J. (2005) *Collapse*, London: Allen Lane

Duffy, J. (2005) *Regeneration through Community Leadership*, in Bond, K. and Farrar, M. (eds) *What are we Learning About Community Leadership in Networks?*, Nottingham: NCSL

Edgar, D. (2001) *The Patchwork Nation*, Sydney: HarperCollins Publishers

Ellis, H. (2004) *Sweetness and Light*, London: Sceptre

ESRC Research Briefing (2000) *An ESRC Research Programme on Children 5–16: Growing into the 21st century*, London: ESRC

Field, J. (2003) *Social Capital*, London: Routledge

Freire, P. (1972) *Pedagogy of the Oppressed*, London: Penguin Books

Freire, P. (1994) *Pedagogy of Hope*, London: Continuum

Freire, P. (2001) *Pedagogy of Freedom*, Lanham, Md: Rowman & Littlefield

Fullan, M. (1999) *Change Forces*, London: Falmer Press

Fullan, M. (2001) *Leading in a Culture of Change*, San Francisco, Calif: Jossey-Bass

Gardner, H. (2006) *The Development and Education of the Mind*, Abingdon: Routledge

Gelsthorpe, T. and West-Burnham, J. (2003) *Educational Leadership and the Community*, London: Pearson Education

Gladwell, M. (2000) *The Tipping Point*, London: Abacus

Glaeser, E.L., Laibson, D. and Sacerdote, B. (2002) 'An economic approach to social capital', *The Economic Journal*, 112, 437–458

Gilchrist, A. (2004) *The Well-Connected Community: A networking approach to community development*, London: The Policy Press

Godfrey, V. (2005) *Building Community Leadership*, in Bond, K. and Farrar, M. (eds) *What are we Learning About Community Leadership in Networks?*, Nottingham: NCSL

Graham, P. (2000) *The Two Worlds: Health and education* (lecture presented to the Royal Children's Hospital) Royal Children's Hospital Education Institute Annual Report, Melbourne, Australia

Halpern, D. (2005) *Social Capital*, Cambridge: Polity Press

Hargreaves, A. and Fink, D. (2006) *Sustainable Leadership*, San Francisco, Calif: Jossey-Bass

Hargreaves, D. (2003) *Education Epidemic*, London: DEMOS

Herzberg, F. (1966) *Work and the Nature of Man*, Cleveland, Oh: World Publishing

Hirschmann, A. (1984) *Getting Ahead Collectively: Grassroots experiences in Latin America*, New York: Pergamon Press

HM Government (2003) *Every Child Matters*, London: The Stationery Office

HM Government (2005) *The Common Core of Skills and Knowledge for the Children's Workforce*, Nottingham: DfES Publications

Hock, D. (1999) *Birth of the Chaordic Age*, San Francisco, Calif: Berrett-Koehler Publishers, Inc.

Holm, B. (1990) *The Dead Get by With Everything*, Minneapolis, Minn, Milkweed Editions

Home Office Community Cohesion Unit (2004) *Community Cohesion Education Standards for Schools*, The Home Office: London

House of Commons Work and Pensions Committee Report (2004) *Child Poverty in the UK*, London: HMSO

Hutton, W. (1995) *The State We're In*, London: Vintage

Huxham, C. and Vangen, S. (2004) *Managing to Collaborate*, London: Routledge

Institute for Educational Leadership (2001) *Education and Community Building: connecting two worlds*, www.communityschools.org/Toolkit/combuild.pdf

Johnson, K. (2004) *Children's Voices: Pupil leadership in primary schools*, Nottingham: NCSL

Johnson, S. (2001) *Emergence*, London: The Penguin Press

Kelley, T. (2005) *The Ten Faces of Innovation*, New York: Doubleday

Lownsbrough, H. and O'Leary, D. (2005) *The Leadership Imperative*, London: DEMOS

Marmot, M. (2005) *Status Syndrome*, London: Bloomsbury

Martin, P. (2005) *Making Happy People*, London: Fourth Estate

Meek, S. (2006) *Social Mobility: Narrowing educational and social class attainment gaps*, London: DfES

Mental Health Foundation Conference Centre (2006) *Ground Rules*, www.connects.org.uk/conferences/main.asp?showItemID=169&codeItemID=

Monbiot, G. (2004) *The Age of Consent*, London: Harper Perennial

Montuori, A. and Conti, I. (1993) *From Power to Partnership: Creating the future of love, work and community*, San Francisco, Calif: Harper

Morrison, K. (2002) *School Leadership and Complexity Theory*, London: RoutledgeFalmer

Moss, M., Petrie, P.P. and Poland, G. (1999) *Rethinking School: Some international perspectives*, Joseph Rowntree Foundation & NYA, Leicester: Youth Work Press

Mount, F. (2004) *Mind the Gap*, London: Short Books

Mulgan, G. (2000) *The Prospect for Social Renewal*, Paris: OECD

National College for School Leadership (2004a) *Future Sight Tool Kit*, www.ncsl.org.uk/research/research_activities/randd-future-index.cfm

National College for School Leadership (2004b) www.ncsl.org.uk/communityleadership/communityleadership

National College for School Leadership (2005a) 'Is there a place for parents in schools?', *LDR*, September, 18: 42–43

National College for School Leadership, (2005b) *What are we Learning about Community Leadership in Networks?*, Nottingham: NCSL

National College for School Leadership (2005c) 'With a little help from our friends', *LDR*, November

National College for School Leadership (2006a) *ECM Why it Matters to Leaders*, Nottingham: NCSL

National College for School Leadership (2006b) *Working Together Helping Community Leadership Work in Practice*, Nottingham: NCSL

Neuberger, J. (2005) *The Moral State We're In*, London: HarperCollins

Noddings, N. (1992) *The Challenge to Care in Schools: An alternative approach to education*, New York: Teachers' College Press

Noddings, N. (2002) *Educating Moral People*, New York: Teachers College Press

OECD (2005) *Think Scenarios, Rethink Education*, Paris: OECD/CERI

OECD PISA (2001) *Knowledge and Skills for Life: First results of PISA 2000*; Paris: OECD

Office of the Children's Commissioner for England (2006) *Annual Report 2005/06*, London: The Stationary Office

Ofsted (2003) *National Summary Data Report for Primary Schools 2003 Data*, London: Ofsted

Owen, H, (1997) *Open Space Technology: A User's Guide*, San Francisco, Calif: Berrett–Kochler

Paton, R. and Vangen, S. (2004) *Understanding and Developing Leadership in Multi–agency Children and Family Teams*, London: DfES

Phillips, C. (2002) *Socrates Café*, New York: W.W. Norton

PISA (2000) 'Student engagement at school', *Results from 2000*, OECD: www.oecd.org

Power, M. (2004) *The Risk Management of Everything*, London: DEMOS

Power, S., Warren, S., Gillborn, D., Clark, A., Thomas, S. and Code, K. (2002) *Education in Deprived Areas: Outcomes, inputs and processes*, London: Institute of Education

Power, S., Whitty, G. and Wisby, E. (2006) *The Educational and Career Trajectories of Assisted Place Holders*, London: The Sutton Trust

Preskill, S., Otero, G. and Vermilya, L. (2000) *Skills for Democracy*, Cheltenham, Victoria: Hawker Brownlow

Putnam, R.D. (2000) *Bowling Alone*, New York: Simon & Schuster

Putnam, R. (2003) *Better Together*, New York: Simon & Schuster

Rutter, M., Maughan, B., Mortimore, P. and Ouston, J. (1979) *Fifteen Thousand Hours*, London: Open Books Publishing

Rezolv (2004) *George Green's: Making Every Child Matter*, Nottingham: NCSL

Sacks, J. (2000) *The Politics of Hope*, London: Vintage

Schaeffer, J. (1996) *The Stone People, Living Together in a Different World*, Waterloo: Forsyth Publications

Schorr, L.B. (1997) *Common Purpose: Strengthening Families and Neighborhoods to Rebuild America*, New York: Doubleday

Search Institute (2000) *Asset Building*, www.search-institute.org

Senge, P., Cabron-McCabe, N., Lucas, T., Smith, B., Dutton, J. and Kleiner, A. (2000) *Schools that Learn*, London: Nicholas Brealey Publishing

Sergiovanni, T. (2001) *Leadership: What's in it for schools?*, London: RoutledgeFalmer

Shelley, S. (2005) 'Working towards community leadership', in Bond, K. and Farrar, M. (eds) *What are we Learning About Community Leadership in Networks?*, Nottingham: NCSL

Silins, H. and Mulford, B. (2002) *Leadership and School Results*, in Leithwood, K. and Hallinger, P. (eds) *Second International Handbook of Educational Leadership and Administration*, Norwell, Ma: Kluwer Academic Press

Sixth Kilbrandon Child Care Lecture (2004) www.scotland.gov.uk/Publications/2004/04/19203/35595

Skilbeck, M. (1970) *Dewey*, London: Collier Macmillan

Smith, J., Hattan, R., Cannon, J., Edwards, J., Wilson, N. and Wurst, S. (2000) *Listen to Me, I'm Learning: Early school learning in South Australian Secondary Schools*, Adelaide: Department of Education and Children's Services

Sorrell, J. and Sorrell, F. (2005) *Joined Up Design for Schools*, London: Merrell

Standing Conference for Community Development (SCCD) (2001) *Strategic Framework for Community Work*, Sheffield: SCCD

The Sutton Trust Report (2005) *Rates of Eligibility for Free School Meals at the Top State Schools*, London: Sutton Trust

Trade Union of Education in Finland (2006) *The Teacher's Professional Ethics*, Trade Union of Education in Finland, www.OAJ.FI

Trevino, Y. and Trevino, R. (2004) *Mutual Assistance: Galvanizing the Spirit of Reciprocity in Communities*, Foundation Consortium for Califfornia's Children and Youth, www.foundationconsortium.org

Wainwright, H. (2003) *Reclaim the State*, London: Verso

Warren, M.R. (2005) 'Communities and schools: a new view of urban education reform', *Harvard Education Review*, 74 (2), 133–175

Weller, S. (2005) *Managing the Move to Secondary School: Children's relationships with social capital*, British–Finnish Seminar on Social Capital, London 10–11 November

Weisbord, M. and Janoff, S. (2000) *Future Search: An Action Guide to Finding Common Ground in Organizations and Communities*, San Francisco, Calif: Berrett-Koehler

Wenger, E. (1998) *Communities of Practice*, Cambridge: Cambridge University Press

Whalley, M. (2002) *Creative Waves: Discussion paper on future schools BERA 2002*, Nottingham: NCSL

Wheatley, M.J. (2002) *Turning to One Another*, San Francisco, Calif: Berrett-Koehler

Wheatley, M. and Crinean, G. (2004) *Solving not Attacking Complex Problems. A five state approach based on an ancient practice*, www.margaretwheatley.com

Wheatley, M.J. and Kellner-Rogers, M. (1998) 'The promise and paradox of community', in Hesselbein, F., Goldsmith, M., Beckhard, R. and Schubert, R.F. (eds) *The Community of the Future*, San Francisco, Calif: Jossey-Bass

Wilkinson, R. (2005) *The Impact of Inequality*, New York: The New Press

W.K. Kellogg Foundation and The Healthcare Forum (2000) *Sustaining Community Based Initiatives*, www.wkkf.org

Woodward, W. (2003) 'Poverty hits exam success', *The Guardian*, 21 April

Zohar, D. (1997) *Rewiring the Corporate Brain*, San Francisco, Calif: Berrett-Koehler

Index